THE HUMAN REMAINS
FROM THE TOMB OF
TUT'ANKHAMŪN

TUT'ANKHAMŪN'S TOMB SERIES

General Editor: J. R. HARRIS

V

THE HUMAN REMAINS FROM THE TOMB OF TUT'ANKHAMŪN

BY

F. FILCE LEEK

OXFORD

PRINTED FOR THE GRIFFITH INSTITUTE

AT THE UNIVERSITY PRESS

BY VIVIAN RIDLER

1972

© *Griffith Institute, Oxford 1972*

PRINTED IN GREAT BRITAIN

TO THE MEMORY OF

WARREN R. DAWSON

WHOSE HELPFUL ENCOURAGEMENT

WAS ALWAYS

FREELY AVAILABLE

ACKNOWLEDGEMENTS

SINCE Howard Carter left so few notes on the human remains found in the tomb of Tut'ankhamūn, the writing of this fascicle would not have been possible had not Professor and Mrs. W. Brian Emery remembered during a lunch-time discussion at the Egyptian Exploration Society's excavation house at Saqqāra the existence of a package of Derry's notes and manuscripts. To them I offer most grateful thanks, and the debt is further increased by Professor Emery's having given permission for them to be used in any way best suited to the present purpose. I should also like to record my appreciation of the help given by Dr. Duncan R. Derry and Mrs. Helen Bryce-Smith, son and daughter of the late Professor D. E. Derry, through whose kindness certain other manuscripts came into my possession.

I have received helpful information from many authorities concerning those momentous days in 1922 following the discovery of the tomb, and am particularly indebted to Professor W. B. Emery, Dr. I. E. S. Edwards, Dr. Kenneth Oakley, and T. G. H. James for interesting comments. To Dr. Peter K. Gray, authority on the X-raying of mummies, to Dr. Mark Patterson and to Mr. Alec Benjamin I am obliged for information on various aspects of mummification and pathology. Any questions asked of Dr. Zaky Iskander, Alfred Lucas's successor in the Department of Antiquities, have been answered fully, and for this too I am very grateful.

Miss Helen Murray and Miss Fiona Strachan, both of the staff of the Griffith Institute, Ashmolean Museum, Oxford, have always been sympathetically helpful during my numerous visits to the Institute to consult material there. My thanks are also due to Eleanor F. Wedge, Wilbour Librarian of The Brooklyn Museum, E. H. Cornelius, Librarian of the Royal College of Surgeons, and Eric J. Freeman, Sub-Librarian of The Wellcome Institute of the History of Medicine, for numerous library services.

Through the kind permission of Professor R. G. Harrison, I was a member of the investigating team during the skeletal examination of the mummy of Tut'ankhamūn in 1968, and was then able to gather information at first hand.

My last and most grateful acknowledgement is to my wife, whose constant aim has been the improvement, in its widest sense, of all aspects of the publication.

CONTENTS

INTRODUCTION

WHEN his workmen uncovered the first of the sixteen steps that led to the burial of Tutʿankhamūn, Howard Carter could have had little realization of the magnitude of the task that awaited him. Yet no one who reads the three volumes of his book, *The Tomb of Tut·ankh·Amen*, can fail to be impressed by his enthusiasm for this gigantic work, and by the infinite knowledge and patience he brought to it. His task consisted of sorting, identifying, describing, preserving, and removing to places of safety the priceless treasures that were found, and while this may readily be appreciated from reading the published account, it is all the more vividly understood when consulting the detailed notes made at the time, and now in the archives of the Griffith Institute. It is these notes, arranged in the main as a card catalogue, that form the basis of the Tutʿankhamūn's Tomb Series, in which this fascicle appears.

In spite of his breadth of knowledge and the wide experience of Egyptology he had acquired during more than twenty-five years in the field, Carter fully realized the necessity to enlist the help of others with special skills in different disciplines. In addition to the assistance of A. C. Mace and A. R. Callender, he therefore sought the aid of James Henry Breasted, Alan H. Gardiner, Percy E. Newberry, the photographer Harry Burton, Alfred Lucas, and Douglas E. Derry, all of whom gave freely of their time and expertise. Unfortunately, however, none of these scholars published the full results of his work, apart from the summaries in the appendices to Carter's volumes, and it is with the object of collating all the existing information about the mummy of Tutʿankhamūn, and to make it available for future study that I have prepared this monograph. It is hoped that some light may be thrown on certain obscurities, and that the many difficulties inherent in the original investigation will be clearly appreciated by students and critics, especially those who think that other methods and techniques should have been employed.

As mentioned above, it is Carter's card inventory that is the foundation for the present series of fascicles, but unfortunately he made very few notes on the subject of the human remains found in the tomb, preferring to leave such detail to Derry. For this reason it has been necessary to seek elsewhere in order to fill in some of the gaps in the published report in CARTER–MACE, II, pp. 143–61 (Appendix I).[1] The most important source of additional information has naturally been the collection of Derry's manuscript notes, including the detailed report now quoted in full. Some interesting facts have also been gathered from Carter's day-to-day diary, which, while it does not add to our knowledge of the human remains, serves none the less to illuminate some of the fascinating, but often frustrating and perplexing problems connected with the discovery.

[1] The way in which Derry there presented his information and conclusions is to be understood in the light of Carter's injunction expressed in a letter written from Luxor on 11 July 1926: '. . . the only thing I ask is that the text be of a kind comprehensible to the layman and the man in the street.'

EXTRACTS FROM
HOWARD CARTER'S DIARY

ALTHOUGH meticulous notes were made of virtually all the objects found in the tomb, Carter did not concern himself with the human remains, the recording of which he left to the two doctors who performed the examination, Douglas E. Derry and Saleh Bey Hamdi. Nor does he seem to have kept any systematic account of the methods employed to remove the royal mummy from its golden coffin. There are many relevant observations, however, in Carter's day-to-day notebooks, the entries in which are for the most part written in pencil, but are still perfectly legible. Like his card catalogue, these notebooks are preserved in the archives of the Griffith Institute. It is not proposed to transcribe the relevant entries in full, since much of the comment is devoted to objects found within the mummy wrappings, but merely to extract the passages relating to the royal mummy.[1]

Oct. 1st 1925. 'Saw Edgar at the Cairo Museum. Arranged with him for the electric light at the Tombs of the Kings to start from Oct. 11th. I also conveyed to him my programme for this season's work (1925–26), and the necessity of making the examination of the Royal Mummy as early as possible, mentioning that the arrangement was for it to take place on or about the 25th of Oct., when Prof. Douglas Derry and Saleh Bey Hamdi would assist. That this scientific examination should be carried out as quietly and reverently as possible, but that I should delay re-wrapping the mummy until I knew whether the Ministers would like [to] inspect the royal remains.'

Oct. 13th. [The lid of the outer coffin was raised] . . . 'revealing a second anthropoid coffin, covered with a thin gossamer linen sheet, darkened and decayed . . .'

Note: 'The only ominous feature is that parts of the second coffin visible through the linen covering, show distinct efflorescence incrusted upon the inlay and surface gold-work and [a] tendency of swelling here and there. This is certainly disconcerting, as it suggests at some time the existence of humidity, possibly from the mummy of the King, wrapped and placed in the coffin before being perfectly dry. If this is the case its preservation will, I fear, not be so good as might have been hoped for.'

Oct. 18th. 'This whole morning was occupied devising the best means for solving the problem of removing this very closely fitting coffin [i.e. the second coffin] from the outer shell, without injuring the very delicate inlay upon its surfaces, that have already suffered from imprisoned humidity, probably at the time of the burial, a condition which becomes more marked as each covering is removed.'[2]

---

[1] The extracts are quoted verbatim, with a very few minor additions enclosed in square brackets [ ]. Passages within the same quotation marks are continuous, the omission of only one or two words being shown by dots . . . Longer omissions are denoted by the closing of the quotation before such dots, and extracts from separate paragraphs are quoted in isolation. Substantial omissions before and after the passages cited are not indicated. [Ed.]

[2] A similar note is entered on 19 Oct., referring there to . . . 'humidity either from the Royal Mummy or the wood imprisoned in all probability at the time of the burial . . .'

Oct. 20th. 'The raising of a lid of a coffin or [the] lifting [of] the coffin itself seems a comparatively simple job; but when one realises that it is deep down in the interior of a sarcophagus where it fits quite closely, that it is in a very fragile condition, that it is immensely heavy, that the overhead room in the chamber is very limited, and that one does not even know whether its wood is sufficiently well preserved to bear its own weight, the reader will perhaps begin to realise what an anxious work it really is.'

Oct. 24th. 'The first part of this morning was occupied by Burton making photographic records of the third coffin . . .'

'It was not until these photographic records were made [that I was] able to remove the linen covering and inspect for the first time the coffin itself. The removal of the coverings was a simple operation as compared to others we have had to face, but it disclosed an astonishing fact—namely that this third coffin is made of solid gold. This accounts for the great weight which has been a source of surprise since the nest of coffins was first lifted out from the sarcophagus, and which diminished so little even when we had removed the outer coffin and the lid of the second coffin, and even at this stage it is as much as eight strong men can lift.' [The coffin is briefly described] . . . 'but the most part of the detail is hidden by a black lustrous coating due to pouring over the coffin a libation in great quantity. As a result this unparalleled monument (coffin) is stuck fast to the interior of the second coffin—the consolidated material of the libation filling up the space between the two coffins almost to the level of the lid of the third one. To extricate this third coffin will be a very tedious and arduous task.'

'The libation referred to is doubtless the principal cause of the signs of humidity encountered in the various outer coffins already dealt with.'

Oct. 26th. 'It was found that the lid of the third coffin was pinned to its shell in the same manner as the other two coffins—namely by means of ten (gold) pins which cannot possibly be extracted as the coffin now stands. The oily or fatty substance of the libation, probably mixed with a wood pitch, was found to be still viscid under the surface, where it is in fairly large quantity.'

Oct. 30th. 'The more one examines the external wrappings of the mummy the more evident it becomes that at least the outer bandages are completely deteriorated, one might say carbonized, from the action of the libation that had been poured over it. One's only hope is that we shall find the wrappings in better condition after several thicknesses have been removed.'

Oct. 31st. 'All the movable objects upon the exterior of the mummy were removed today. I then attempted to remove the mummy and mask from the coffin, but found that unfortunately both were stuck fast to the bottom of the coffin, and could not be under the present conditions raised out without using great force, endangering both the royal remains and that finely wrought mask. The libation that was poured over the body had consolidated at the bottom and stuck them fast. My one hope now is that the heat of the sun may soften it sufficiently so as to enable one to gradually free it and raise it. In fact, unless some other expedient is discovered, we shall have to make the examination as it lies within the two coffins.'

'With regard to the libation it would appear from the materials that it is composed of seemingly fatty or oily substance mixed with (?) wood-pitch—that it is more an anointment than a libation.

This liquid no doubt was applied in [a] religious ceremony for the consecration of the dead King before appearing before the Great God (Osiris) of the underworld. It is particularly noticeable that on both the third coffin and the mummy the head and feet have been carefully avoided even though the feet of the first coffin were anointed with a similar material.'[1]

Nov. 1st. 'Removed the Royal Mummy to No. 15. It took ten men to bring it out of the tomb and carry it up. Placed in the sun for a few hours' . . . 'Heat of the sun not sufficient today to make any real impression upon the pitch-like material which has stuck fast the mummy and coffins.'

Nov. 2nd. 'Found that the heat of the sun was of no avail in freeing the mummy from its coffin. In consequence, the examination of the Royal Mummy must necessarily take place as it lies.'

Nov. 4th. [The shell of the first coffin was raised out of the sarcophagus] . . . 'This was done by means of pulleys attached to the overhead scaffolding and to metal eyelets fixed into the thickness of the upper edge of the coffin. It was then raised sufficiently above the sarcophagus to enable us to pass a wooden tray under it, upon which it was lowered, and then lifted out into the antechamber. It proves to be a great weight, and has suffered considerably from humidity in past ages causing the gold work upon gesso to bulge and become completely detached from the basic wood. Fortunately it can be repaired and made good by careful filling in the interstices with hot paraffin wax.'

Nov. 5th. 'Everything is now ready for the examination of the Royal Mummy, which I trust will occur next week.'

Nov. 9th. 'Prepared Royal Mummy for examination.' . . . 'Arranged for Lacau, Derry and Saleh Bey—arriving Wednesday 11th.'

Nov. 11th. 'Today has been a great day in the history of archaeology, I might also say in the history of archaeological discovery, and a day of days for one who after years of work, excavating, conserving and recording has longed to see in fact what previously has only been conjectural.' [There follows a list of those present.][2] 'As aforementioned the mummy of the King could not without considerable damage be removed from the coffin, [and] the examination had necessarily to take place as it lay.

10.35 a.m. In consequence of the fragile and powdery nature of the outer layers of the wrappings, the whole of the exposed surface of the mummy except the mask was painted over with melted paraffin wax of such a temperature that it chiefly congealed as a thin coating on the surface and did not penetrate the decayed wrappings more than a very short distance.

As soon as the wax had cooled, Dr. Derry made a longitudinal incision down the centre of the outer wrappings to just below the depth to which the wax had penetrated, thus enabling the

---

[1] These thoughts had arisen because of references to anointing in Psalms 45:7; 92:10; Isaiah 61:3; Mark 14:8.

[2] See Plate 1. Derry himself is facing the camera in another group published in *The Illustrated London News*, 6 February 1926, p. 234.

During the years immediately following the opening of the tomb, considerable publicity was given to the so-called 'curse' of Tut'ankhamūn, both in this country and elsewhere, and belief in it has not yet entirely disappeared. Surely if such a 'curse' existed it should have applied above all to the man who made the first anatomical examination of the dead pharaoh. But no ill events befell Derry, whose life span in fact far exceeded the normal expectancy. According to *The Lives of the Fellows of the Royal College of Surgeons*, 'Derry's years of retirement were spent in a sixteenth century cottage, Little Linden Cottage, Radwinter, Essex. He was still upright and alert until his sudden death on 20th February 1961 at the age of 87.' It may be added that the implication, so frequently found, that an inscription threatening evil consequences to intruders exists at the entrance of the tomb is entirely without foundation.

consolidated outer layers of the wrappings to be removed in large pieces, the under bandages which were very voluminous were found to be equally decayed and fragile, in fact, the deeper and nearer the body, the worse the condition.'

'After removing the outer layer of wrappings, it was still found impossible to withdraw the mummy from the mask and coffin, the pitch-like material having collected in large quantity underneath. It was decided therefore to remove layer by layer the remainder of the wrappings. Here and there where the linen was slightly better preserved it was possible to recognize that the mode of binding was as usually practised upon mummies of the New Empire. Here and there were a number of tightly wrapped pads of linen; beyond these facts, little else could be recognized, the linen being reduced to the consistency of soot.'

'It is to be much regretted that the wrappings were found in such critical condition—a condition preventing any reliable record of them, even their approximate system of binding.'

Nov. 12th. 'The proceedings recommenced 8.15 a.m. by Mr. Burton taking further records—duplicating yesterday afternoon's photographs—as we had decided to reverse the position of the coffin on account of the light.

Further layers of decayed wrappings were carefully removed from the lower part of the mummy...'

'This enabled the body to be bared down to the skin, from the top of the abdomen to the feet. The feet were fitted with gold sandals, the toes with gold stalls, upon the right ankle was a gold wire circlet. Between the shin bones near towards the ankles was a small amulet of gold, beads, and (?) hair. When this portion of the remains of the King [was] uncovered, i.e. his legs, pubis and abdomen, it was manifest that we were dealing with the mortal remains of a young person—and a more detailed medical examination to follow will determine with certainty his exact age.

Throughout these proceedings the wrappings though much rotted and carbonized, showed evidence of having once been of fine cambric like quality. Again, whenever it was possible to discern details of [the] method of wrapping, the evidence was suggestive of hastiness—that was the concensus of opinion among the scientific element present.

So as to complete this stage of [the] examination the afternoon was devoted to uncovering the right arm and hand which was flexed across the abdomen . . .'

'Near the flesh of the King the wrappings were nothing more than charred powder.'

Nov. 13th. 'The lower limbs and body having been thoroughly cleaned, Drs. Derry and Saleh Bey proceeded to take as many measurements as it was possible at this stage, and on account of its fragile condition the whole of the exposed parts were saturated with hot paraffin-wax.

Following this the last portions of the wrappings were removed from the left forearm and hand, exposing another important group of bracelets as well as a group of finger-rings.'

'During the afternoon the above objects were removed, and further anatomical examination was made.

The soft tissues of the body were found to be all in a very brittle and carbonized condition.

Further than the above discoveries there is little to add today, owing to the greater part of the day being occupied in making archaeological, anatomical and photographic notes.

Though we have only reached as far as the forearms of the young King, the upper portion and the head having yet to be examined, 52 groups of objects—personal and religious jewellery—have been discovered. . . .'

Nov. 14th. 'M. Lacau and the two doctors together [with] the inspectors arrived at Valley 8.30 a.m., when we recommenced work.'

'The lower part of the body and limbs having been completely bared and thoroughly examined, as well as photographic records taken, we were able to proceed with the uncovering of the upper part of the trunk of [the] body as far as the shoulders.'

'The result of Drs. Derry and Saleh Bey's study of the boney frame of the mummy, so far exposed, has enabled them to give a definite pronouncement as to the age of Tut-Ankh-Amen. This controversial question has now been settled and his age definitely fixed between the limits of 17 to nineteen years of age. As soon as the upper parts of the mummy are examined an even more precise statement will be possible.'

Nov. 15th. 'It is now five days since the examination of the mummy was begun, and by this afternoon we have reached only as far as the neck, having completed the investigation from the feet thus far.'

'Under the back of the mummy across the scapulae, a series of sections of ornament lying face downwards and in great part stuck fast to bottom of coffin, being embedded in the pitch-like material.'

'All that remains to be done is the examination of the head of the mummy, which we were obliged to leave until the last due to its being completely covered by its golden mask fast adhering to the coffin.

The two doctors today have been able to definitely declare the age of the young King to be about eighteen years.'

Nov. 16th. 'The whole of today's work was concentrated upon the head of the mummy.'

'It was found that like the body of the King the back of the head was stuck (in this case) to the mask—so firmly that it would require a hammer and chisel to free it. Eventually we used hot knives for the purpose with success.'

'These objects [i.e. objects around the neck] recorded and removed, it was possible after applying of hot knives, to withdraw the head from its mask.

Some of the outer bandages of the top of the head remained adhering to the interior of the mask, thus exposing a double rope-like "lawaya" encircling the crown of the head, made of a (?) fibrous material tightly bound with string. This had slipped down slightly during the operation of withdrawing the head from [the] mask.'

'Sufficient of the head of the King was exposed today to show us that Tut-Ankh-Amen was of a type exceedingly refined and cultured. The face has beautiful and well formed features. The head shows strong structural resemblance to Akh-en-aten' . . . 'a resemblance in character which makes one inclined to seek a blood relationship . . .'[1]

Nov. 18th. 'Upon the head was placed a sort of skull-cap of fine linen . . .'

'This actual skull-cap of the thinnest cambric fabric having [a] device of four uraei worked with very fine faience and gold beads . . . fits closely to the crown of the head. As it would have been practically impossible to remove this device owing to its fragile nature and minuteness of work, it was consolidated with paraffin wax and left in place.[2]

Upon the top of the head of the King was an enormous pad some centimetres in height, of linen

---

[1] For this comparison, cf. below, p. 15, n. 1. [Ed.]   [2] Cf. Plate XI.

wads and bandages wrapped in the manner of a modern surgical head bandage.[1] This was of a conical form and its shape was suggestive of a crown. The linen was in this case in far better preservation than any hitherto found upon the mummy.'

'After photographic records are made of the King's remains, these will be reverently re-wrapped and returned to the sarcophagus.

M. Lacau, who was present during the whole of this examination, left today for Cairo, taking with him a final archaeological bulletin as well as that of the two doctors Derry and Saleh Bey.

As will be seen from the above bulletin of the various discoveries made there were 97 separate groups of objects within the wrappings of the mummy. Some of these groups included many individual objects.'

Nov. 19th. 'Final measurements were taken of the head of the King, some photos of certain bones, and thus the examination was completed.

Saleh Bey and Derry left after lunch.'

Nov. 20th. 'The whole of today was occupied in cleaning and restoring the gold coffin No. 155.'

Nov. 21st–23rd. 'Spent on cleaning and restoring objects found upon the mummy, as well as the lid of the third coffin which is now complete.'

Nov. 27th–Dec. 14th. 'It was a terrible job extricating the third innermost coffin of gold from the interior of the inlaid wooden second coffin, where it was firmly fixed by the congealed anointing substance. Originally something like two buckets full of the liquid had been poured over the third coffin, the main part of which had flowed between and filled up the space between the two coffins, where it dried and became a solid mass. In the same manner the mask of the King was stuck to the interior of the third innermost coffin.

It was found that this pitch-like material could be melted under great heat, and that was really the only means of successfully getting the coffins and mask apart. Thus, so as to apply sufficient heat as was necessary without causing damage . . ., the third coffin was completely lined with plates of zinc which would not melt under a temperature of 500 centigrade. We then reversed the coffins by turning them upside down upon the trestles, covered the outside (second) coffin with heavy wet blankets for protection against fire, and placed under the hollow of the third coffin primus paraffin lamps burning at full blast. The temperature was naturally carefully watched so that it did not exceed the melting point of the zinc plates. It took some three hours before any real effect in the way of movement took place. The moment signs of movement became apparent, the lamps were turned out and the coffins left suspended upon the trestles when after an hour they began slowly to fall apart—the movement at first almost imperceptible owing to the tenacity of the material which when heated was of an exceedingly plastic nature and of the consistency of thick treacle, which even when the coffins came apart was very difficult to remove—even with quantities of various solvents—among which the final cleaning was done by means of acetone.

The mask was also a difficult undertaking—the inlay had become unstuck from the heat applied to free it from the coffin. It took many days for final cleaning and I am still replacing the numerous pieces of glass and stone inlay that came away.

[1] Plate x, bottom.

Extricating numbers of small beads and parts of objects that were embedded in the pitch-like material collected under the mummy was also a very tiresome and long job.'

Dec. 16th–31st. 'Completed the gold coffin 255 and gold mask 256 *a*.'

Dec. 31st. 'Left for Cairo with Lucas with 3 cases containing the coffin 255 and mask 256 *a* and handed them over to the Museum.'

1926

Oct. 9th. 'Cleaned and prepared laboratory for work to begin to-morrow, namely, (1) completing the Royal Mummy for final reburial, (2) completing the first (outermost) coffin to receive the mummy.'

Oct. 10th. 'Lucas and I commenced real work this morning; Lucas upon cleaning and reparation of the first (outermost) coffin shell; myself upon the final touches of the King's mummy before reburial when we open the tomb.'

From the foregoing notes, and more so from the diary as a whole, it is easy to follow Carter's devouring passion for all the many treasures and artifacts found in the tomb and within the sarcophagus. It is also possible to feel his lack of interest in the human remains, except as regards the king's facial resemblance to previous rulers, and his probable age at the time of his death.

This lack of interest is further emphasized by the unemotional entry in his daily diary for 23 October 1926 which reads: 'The first outermost coffin containing the King's Mummy, finally rewrapped, was lowered into the sarcophagus this morning. We are now ready to begin upon the investigation of the Store Room [i.e. the Treasury].'

THE ANATOMICAL REPORT ON
THE ROYAL MUMMY

THE most important of Derry's manuscripts held by Professor Emery, is that entitled:

'Anatomical Report on the Mummy of King TutAnkhAmon', by Dr. D. E. Derry and Dr. Saleh Bey Hamdi.

This represents the fullest extant account of the examination, and contains technical information additional to that already published. It is therefore printed in full.[1]

REPORT ON THE UNCOVERING OF THE MUMMY OF KING TUTANKHAMON.[2]

The examination of the mummy of King TutAnkhAmon was begun on the 11th of November 1925. When first seen the mummy was lying in the coffin to which it was firmly fixed by some resinous or pitch-like material which had been poured over the mummy while it was lying in the coffin. Over the head and shoulders and reaching well down over the chest was a gold mask, which is an effigy of the King's face, head-dress, and collar. This could not be removed as it also was stuck to the bottom of the coffin. The mummy was enclosed in a sheet which was held in position by bandages passing round ankles, knees, hips, and (?) shoulders. These were all in a state of extreme fragility and crumbled at a touch. It was clear that no sort of orderly unwrapping was possible and as all operations had to be conducted with the mummy *in situ* it was thought well to strengthen the upper layers with melted paraffin wax in order that they might be incised and turned back with less disturbance. This was done and an incision was carried down the middle line of the mummy wrappings from the lower edge of the mask to the feet. This penetrated only a few millimetres and the two flaps so produced were turned outwards.

A number of objects came in view included in the layers of bandages and thereafter it became necessary to remove the latter piecemeal to expose the objects in order that they might be photographed before being touched and numerically recorded. Throughout the course of this part of the work which was necessarily slow, the increasing state of disintegration of the wrappings was noticeable. These in many places were reduced to dust, largely owing to the carbonization brought about by a sort of spontaneous combustion due to enclosed humidity combined with heat.

The first parts of the actual body to be exposed were the lower limbs from the knees downwards. The feet were provided with gold sandals put on after the first few layers of bandages had been applied, and after each toe had been separately wrapped and fitted with a gold sheath over the wrappings. The bar of the sandal passed between the great and second toes.

The skin of the legs was of a greyish white colour, very brittle and exhibiting numerous cracks. Examination of a piece of this showed that it consisted not only of the skin but of all the soft parts

---

[1] The original manuscript has a number of marginal emendations, and certain passages have been marked for abbreviation (?) in Carter's hand. Simple corrections are here incorporated, but nothing of substance has been omitted. [Ed.]

[2] Cf. Plates II–XX, with the accompanying notes (below pp. 27–9).

down to the bone, which was thus laid bare when such a piece came away, the whole thickness of skin and tissues being in this situation not more than two or three millimetres. The fractured edges resembled glue. There is little doubt that this was the result of the combustion referred to above. The left patella and skin covering it could be lifted off and the lower end of the femur was thus exposed, showing the condylar epiphysis which was found to be separate from the shaft and freely movable.

The thighs and lower part of the abdomen were gradually exposed as the objects covering them were removed. The lower limbs appeared very shrunken and attenuated. The abdominal wall was in the same state as that described for the limbs, exhibiting numerous cracks which had broken the wall into small pieces. These came away at a touch and were extremely brittle. The penis surrounded by bandages was in the erect position and measured 50 mm. in length. The scrotum was flattened against the perineum. It was not possible to say whether circumcision had been performed. On the left side of the abdomen was a ragged opening 86 mm. in length, parallel to a line drawn from the umbilicus to the anterior superior iliac spine and an inch above it.[1] This was only exposed after the removal of a carbonized mass of what was apparently resin, and the length of the incision may therefore have been originally greater than is now apparent, owing to the hardness of the adherent mass which made it difficult to define the limits of the wound. The lips of the wound are inverted due to the forcible packing of the abdomen with a mass of linen and resin, now of rock-like hardness. The material had been forced across by the embalmer to the right side and this had caused a marked bulging of the abdominal wall on that side. No pubic hair is visible. The plate of gold or wax so frequently found covering the embalming wound was not present, but an oval plate of gold was found on the left side during the removal of the wrappings included amongst the layers of bandages, and in the neighbourhood of the opening in the abdominal wall.

The upper limbs were flexed at the elbows and the right forearm was resting on the upper part of the abdomen with the hand on the crest of the left ilium. The left forearm lay above it over the lower ribs with the hand lying on the right side of the thorax between this and the right upper arm. Both forearms were loaded with bracelets from the bend of the elbow to the wrist. All the fingers were fitted with gold sheaths *over* the wrappings. As it was found impossible to continue the work of removing the numerous objects still covering the thorax and upper part of [the] abdomen while the chest remained covered by the mask, it was decided to remove the limbs and then endeavour to free the trunk by working beneath it in order to withdraw the mummy from the mask. This was finally accomplished and the removal of the limbs allowed of a more detailed examination of the epiphyses.

The *lower end* of the *femur* came away at the epiphyseal line, showing the cartilaginous surface intact, there being no sign of any commencing union between it and the shaft of the bone.

At the *upper end* of the *femur* the condition of the epiphyses was as follows. The lesser trochanter was fused to the shaft, only a faint impression representing the line of union being visible. The *great trochanter* was almost entirely soldered to the main bone, but on the inner side a definite gap showing the smooth epiphyseal surface could be well seen. The epiphysis of the *head* of the femur was fused to the neck, but the line of union was clearly visible all round.

The *upper* epiphysis of the *tibia* is still separate; the *lower end* appears to be quite fused.

The *upper* epiphysis of the *fibula* is not yet joined to the shaft and was removed revealing the cartilaginous surface. The *lower* end could not be examined as it was still attached to the foot.

[1] Cf. Appendix 1.

The *heads* of both *humeri* are still not united, but the lower epiphyses are completely united including that capping the internal condyle. The left bone exhibits a very large supratrochlear foramen, the right a very small one.

The *head* of the *radius* is fused but the line of union is just visible internally. The *lower end* is absolutely free and came away easily from the shaft bringing the entire hand with it. This enabled the numerous bracelets to be slipped off the forearm. A photograph showing the surfaces of the shaft and its epiphysis with the smooth remains of the cartilage which had united them was taken.

In the *ulna* the cartilage between the shaft and styloid process was still present, but as the rest of the epiphysis to which the styloid process is attached did not come completely away, union *may* have commenced in it, though this is highly improbable as ossification almost invariably begins at the base of the styloid process and proceeds across the ulna and so to the radius.

The *acromion* process of the scapula is not united and cartilaginous islands are still present in the process itself.

The sternal epiphyses of the *clavicles* are, as might be expected, entirely separate from the shaft.

In the *hip bone* the crest of the ilium is separate in its whole length. The ilio-sciatic notch is of male type and there is complete absence of the preauricular groove.

No examination of the body cavity was possible as it was filled completely with a tightly-packed mass of linen caked into a solid block by the resin with which it had apparently been impregnated.

From the condition of the epiphyses above described it would appear that the King was about eighteen years of age at the time of his death. None of the epiphyses that should unite at about the 20th year shows any sign of union. There is evidence that in Egypt the epiphyses tend on the average to unite somewhat earlier than is the rule in Europe. It is found by X-ray examination of persons whose date of birth is known, that the lower epiphysis of the radius begins to unite about 18 and the line of union is distinct at 19, though by that age only the lateral side is, as a rule, still not completely joined to the shaft by bone, ossification spreading, as mentioned above, from the ulnar to the radial side. In King TutAnkhAmon no ossification whatever has begun between shaft and lower end of radius and he might therefore be deemed to be less than 18 on the evidence of modern Egyptians. Against this however we have the complete union of the internal condyle of the humerus and the condition of the upper end of the femur, as well as the lower end of the tibia, all pointing to 18 as being approximately his age.[1]

Bandaging. It was impossible to follow the system of bandaging owing to the state of the wrappings. Numerous wads of linen were found between the layers of bandages, so placed as to fill up the inequalities produced by the numerous objects which were included in the coverings of the mummy. It was noticed that some of the linen was of the nature of the finest cambric, notably that used on the body itself next to the skin and the last bandages applied in completing the wrapping. Most of the inner bandages were of stronger make. All *fingers* and *toes* were bandaged individually and the gold sheaths adjusted over each before the bandage covering the whole hand or foot was applied. In the case of the *feet* the gold sandals were put on at the same stage in order to allow the bar of the sandal to be adjusted between the great and second toes. At one stage folded sheets of linen were placed along the *front of the body* as far as the knees, and these were retained by transverse bandages. In the *perineum* the crossed arrangement of the bandages was easily visible though the method used to produce this arrangement could not be followed out. Over the *thorax* the bandages were made to pass alternately in crossed and transverse layers, the crossed bandages being carried

[1] Cf. Appendix 2.

over one shoulder then round the body and over the opposite shoulder. All the *limbs* were separately wrapped before being enclosed by the bandages which enveloped the body as a whole.

Head. When first exposed the crown of the bandaged head was surrounded by a string which passed twice around the head and served to enclose a circular bandage. This string which somewhat resembled a Beduin head-rope, but of much smaller diameter, was composed of some sort of fibre around which twine had been tightly wound. The circular bandage in its turn held in place a sheet which passed over the head and face. Upon this and over the region of the left eye lay six large blue beads strung together. Beneath this sheet was the diadem enclosed in the bandages which passed alternately across the head and transversely round the face, covering in those dependant parts of the diadem which overlay the ears. A gold band passing round the forehead and above the ears and fastened at the back with a linen tape was removed from beneath a few further turns of bandage. Still further layers but of no great depth covered a gold hawk[1] with outspread wings lying on the crown of the head, while on the forehead was the uraeus, its tail passing directly backwards in the middle line of the head beneath the hawk, the end of the tail being sewn to the bandages over the region of the lambda. After these were removed the bandages in the occipital region and back of neck were gradually lifted revealing the ends of another gold band, which were united by a linen tape, tied in a knot beneath the occiput. When the bandages covering this gold circlet were taken away, the top of the head was seen to be covered by a bead-work arrangement in the form of four serpents, the tails of the two central ones extending back to below the occiput, while the two lateral ones met across the forehead above the gold circlet in the form of a bandeau.

When the face was finally exposed, some resinous material was found plugging the nostrils, and a further layer had been laid over the eyes and between the lips.

The head appeared to be clean-shaved and the skin of the scalp was covered by a whitish substance probably fatty acid. Two abrasions on the skin covering the upper part of the interparietal bone had apparently been caused by the pressure of the diadem (?).[2]

The plugs filling the nostrils and the material laid over the eyes were found by Mr. Lucas to consist of some woven fabric, probably linen, impregnated with resin. Mr. Lucas also examined some whitish spots on the skin over the upper part of the back and shoulders and these proved to be composed of 'common salt with a small admixture of sodium sulphate', in all probability derived from natron used in the embalming process.

The *eyes* were partly open, and were not stuffed in any way. The eyelashes were very long. The cartilage of the *nose* had collapsed. The *upper lip* was everted revealing the large central incisor teeth. The *ears* were small and well made and the lobe of the left ear is perforated by a circular hole measuring 7·5 mm. in diameter. The lobe of the right ear was not found and had probably come away when the bandages were removed. The *skin* of the face was of a greyish colour and very cracked and brittle. On the left cheek just in front of the lobe of the ear is a rounded depression, the skin filling it resembling a scab. Round the circumference of the depression, which had slightly raised edges, the skin was discoloured.

The head when fully uncovered was seen to be very broad and flat-topped (platycephalic) with markedly-projecting occipital region. Even allowing for the shrinkage of the scalp and the loss of the neck muscles this is still remarkable. There is pronounced left occipital bulging and the post-bregmatic region is depressed. The general shape of this head which is very uncommon is so like

---

[1] In fact a vulture. [Ed.]

[2] A marginal note (? by Carter) suggests '? during mummification'.

that of his father-in-law Akhenaton[1] that it is more than probable that there is a close relationship in blood between these two Kings.

The skull cavity was empty except for some resinous material which had been introduced through the nose by breaking down the ethmoid bone.

The right upper and lower wisdom teeth had just erupted the gum and reached to about half the height of the 2nd molar. Those on the left side could not be seen easily, but they appeared to be in the same stage of eruption.

Measurements of Head.

	mm.
Glabello-occipital length	188·0
Maximum breadth	156·5
Basi-bregmatic height	133·0
Auricular height (approx.)	114·0
Frontal breadth (min.)	100·0
Height of face (naso-alveolar)	73·5
Height of face (naso-mental)	118·0
Nose (nasion to lower edge of septum)	54·5
Width (across nostrils)	30·0
Bizygomatic breadth	132·0
Bigonial breadth	100·0
Circumference (over gold band)	553·0
Nasion to between lips	81·0
Between lips to chin	41·0
Ear (right) length	54·5
Ear (right) breadth	broken

The skin or scalp over which the measurements were necessarily made was found to be only 0·5 mm. in thickness. In order to get the actual skull dimensions 1·0 millimetre must be deducted from the lengths and breadths as given above, and the same from the bigonial and bizygomatic breadths. The basi-bregmatic height although probably very close to the actual height had to be measured from a point on the scalp which was estimated as being the site of the bregma and some error may therefore have occurred here. The auricular height can only be considered as an estimate. Under the conditions, it was not possible to be sure either of the lower border of the orbit or the upper margin of the auditory meatus, so that considerable error was possible here. The same is true of the measurements made from the nasion, the position of which could only be estimated, as it was not possible either to see or feel the fronto-nasal junction. The circumference was measured over the gold band mentioned in the description of the head bandages and should probably be reduced by about 6 mm. making the actual measurement 547·0 mm.

[1] Derry is here referring to the human remains cached in the so-called tomb of Queen Tiy (no. 55), which at the time of his writing were generally thought to be those of Akhenaten. He himself was later to undertake an accurate re-examination of these remains, including a reconstruction of the skull (*ASAE*, 31 (1931), pp. 115–19), since when it has come to be recognized that the body cannot have been that of Akhenaten, but was in all probability Smenkhkarēʿ (see latterly R. G. Harrison, *JEA*, 52 (1966), pp. 95–119). [Ed.]

Trunk and limb measurements

	mm.
Between ant. sup. iliac spines	226·0
Between tuberosities of ilia	252·0
Between great trochanters	267·0

All following on *left* side

Length from ant. sup. spine of ilium to internal malleolus	880·0
Length from great trochanter to int. malleolus	830·0
Length from perineum to int. malleolus	760·0
Length from perineum to sole of foot	820·0
Length from top of great trochanter to lower edge of int. condyle of femur	450·0
Length from int. tub. of tibia to internal malleolus	383·0
Length of left femur: max.	465·0
: oblique	464·0
Length of left tibia from edge of ant. surface to malleolus	383·0
Length of leg from ant. surface of inner tub. of tibia to sole	443·0

In following right and left are indicated

Length of humerus: right	323·0
: left	324·5
Length of clavicle: right with epiphysis	142·0
: left minus epiphysis	134·0
Length of radius (right) from head to lower end of shaft *without* epiphysis	239·0
Epiphysis-thickness	7·0
Total length of radius	246·0
Diameter of right acetabulum	51·0
Diameter of head of right femur: vert.	47·0
: trans.	46·5
Diameter of head of left femur: vert.	45·5
: trans.	45·5

Circumference of chest

Over some bead work and remains of linen	635·0

Living height of King as estimated from measurements of femur, tibia, humerus, and radius by Prof. Karl Pearson's Tables = 1·676 metres.

DOUGLAS E. DERRY

Towards the end of the report Derry makes two terse observations: first that the skull was empty except for some resinous material which had been introduced through the nose, and second that the third molar teeth had just erupted the gum.

In order to ascertain that the cranial cavity was empty, the linen plugs filling the nose would have had to be removed and a wire inserted up the nostril. No mention is made of whether the cribriform plate of the ethmoid bone had been pierced through the left or right nostril or through both, or whether or not the nasal septum had been destroyed during this operation. The observation could easily have been made during the skeletal investigation of 1968, but it was considered inadvisable to displace the plugs from the nostrils, though easily removable. Nor does Derry say how he determined that resin had been introduced into the skull; perhaps this was merely assumed because of its weight. What he did not realize is that within the skull (as revealed in the 1968 investigations) there are two areas of resin lying at right angles to each other, of which one must have been poured in through the nose while the body was in a supine position, and the other while it was held vertically and upside down.[1]

Evidence of the degree of development and eruption of the third molar teeth gives almost essential information—and at times precisely the confirmation needed—for estimating the age at death. This is especially true if the event took place before the age of twenty years. The second of Derry's brief observations relates to this, noting that those on the right had erupted through the gum and reached about half the height of the second molar, and that those on the left appeared to have reached the same stage of development.[2]

In this connection there are two indisputable facts to be borne in mind: first that no radiological facilities were available in the tomb (this statement will be confirmed below when reference is made to notes written by Derry), and second that owing to the post-mortem rigidity of muscle fibres it is quite impossible to open the mouth of a mummy to look inside it, without destroying and causing obvious damage to the tissues of the face.

As a member of Professor R. G. Harrison's party that made an anatomical investigation of the remains of the pharaoh in 1968 I fully appreciated this fact, and fearing that a constant electrical supply might not be available in the tomb, I devoted much thought to other forms of energy that would enable a radiographic film to be taken of the teeth. Eventually, with the co-operation of various members of the United Kingdom Atomic Energy Authority, a technique was perfected for obtaining a panoramic dental radiograph by using as a source of energy the radioactive isotope I^{125}. As this nuclide decays with the emission of gamma rays of a low intensity with no beta particles, problems of shielding for induced radioactivity are non-existent, since with such small quantities of the isotope involved no radiation damage can follow its use.

When the time came to start the experiment it was found that the area beneath the chin was covered by a thin layer of shiny, hard, resinous material. Because of its smooth appearance it was considered that it would be extremely brittle, and that to puncture it while inserting the minute bead of the isotope would cause it to fracture in various directions. I was permitted instead to make an exposure from an angle external to the face, but as anticipated the result was a blank exposure. Thus this experiment which could have revealed a complete record of the dental condition of the king was negated, though a certain amount is now known about the teeth, since the conventional radiographs, taken by Harrison with the aid of a portable Siemens X-ray unit, were successful.

To return to Derry, it is quite evident that he gained his information without the use of radiology, and without being able to open the mouth. A probable explanation is that in order to obtain such highly desirable data an incision was made with a sharp scalpel beneath the chin, around the inner

[1] Cf. Plate XXI. It is more probable that the head alone was held vertically and upside down, by forcing it back into this position while keeping the body supine. [Ed.]

[2] On the basis of these observations (confirmed by the lateral head X-ray: Plate XXI), it might appear that Derry's over-all estimate of the age at death (above, p. 13) should be regarded as a maximum.

border of the mandible, and continued upwards until it reached the floor of the mouth. Then, by the insertion of a thin spatula in the region of the symphysis, and pressing the free end upwards, the whole of the tongue and its attachments could be pulled down, thus exposing the inner sides of the teeth. As this is a normal post-mortem examination procedure, it is one with which Derry must without doubt have been conversant. After the examination the tissues would have been replaced, and the whole area beneath the chin covered with a thin layer of resin, thus obliterating all signs of interference.

Such a hypothesis would account for the shiny layer of resin beneath the chin, which had such a clean, fresh appearance, in marked contrast to other areas of resin to be seen on the body, and would also explain the method by which Derry was able to determine the state of eruption of the third molars.

It has already been mentioned that Professor Emery had in his possession a package containing a number of Derry's articles, manuscripts, and notes. Among these are:

A. An untitled MS., a preliminary draft which eventually became Derry's contribution to CARTER–MACE, II.
B. An exercise book, on the front of which is written: 'Notes during examination of mummy of Tut-Ankh-Amon'.

In this latter there are three separate entries, headed:

1. Unwrapping of Mummy of the King Tut-Ankh-Amen. Begun 11/11/25.
2. The examination of the mummy of the King Tut-Ankh-Amon.
3. Thirty lines, written in pencil on the last two pages of the book and untitled.

The first entry was undoubtedly written during the course of the examination and contains the essentials of the final report. It has, however, one variant so important that the paragraph is here quoted in full.

'As it was found impossible to continue the work of removing the numerous objects still covering the thorax and upper part of [the] abdominal wall it was decided to remove the limbs and finally to cut through the trunk above the iliac crests as the latter was firmly glued to the bottom of the coffin. This was done and the lower part of [the] trunk removed. It was now possible to examine the ends of the limbs in detail.'[1]

The corresponding passage in the second entry reads as follows:

'As it was found impossible to continue the work of removing the numerous objects still covering the thorax and the upper part of the abdomen while the chest remained covered by the mask, it was decided to first remove the limbs and then to endeavour to free the trunk by working beneath it, in order to withdraw the mummy from the mask. This was finally accomplished and the removal of the limbs allowed of a more detailed examination of their epiphyses.'[2]

On the last two pages of the exercise book reference is made to the possibilities of the use of X-ray photography. The entry is given as it stands, and will be seen to confirm the statement made above (p. 17).

---

[1] That the trunk was in fact cut through is confirmed by a photograph taken at the time (Plate XII), and may also be seen from the X-ray (Plate XXII).

[2] Cf. the similar wording of the final report (above, p. 12).

'When the mummy of the King was first seen it was found to be firmly glued to the bottom of the gold coffin by dried pitch-like material which had been used as a libation. The mask which reached to the upper part of [the] thorax was also fixed both to the coffin and to the mummy. The removal of the mummy was thus impossible. The employment of X-rays was considered but the facts just recorded as well as the presence of numerous layers of objects of gold, faience etc. covering the body completely as far as the knees, would render the use of the rays utterly futile. A form of spontaneous combustion had destroyed the bandages, and caused the skin and underlying tissues to become extremely thin and brittle. This condition exposed certain of the joints which enabled the age of the King at death to be fairly accurately estimated as about 18 years. He was evidently of slight build. The belief that the statues and effigies of the King were in reality portraits, finds confirmation in the face now exposed.'

From all the above, it is evident that when it was found that the linen wrappings, the mummy, the mask, and the base of the coffin were all intimately bound together by the solidified unguents that had been poured into and over the gold coffin, the dilemma confronting the investigators was so great that if any successful result were to be obtained, the most drastic measures had to be taken. It is a source of great satisfaction that as a consequence of these measures, which involved dismembering the limbs, the epiphyseal unions of many bones were exposed, thus revealing vital age data.

It had been hoped that Derry's anatomical examination would reveal the cause of death, and Carter was bitterly disappointed when this did not prove the case. The latter years of the Eighteenth Dynasty are full of uncertainties for the historian, and he would have welcomed the establishment of such an important fact.

That Derry's examination was exhaustive and competent can be judged from his precise and comprehensive report. Moreover, his inability to give a pronouncement as to the cause of death is not as surprising as might appear. Visible signs upon the external parts of the body which are the result of the causative factor of death are remarkably few.

A violent blow with a mace-head, penetration by an arrow, a thrust from a sharp weapon, or laceration by a wild animal, any of which resulted in immediate death, would leave visible external signs. There are, however, other forms of violence or accident that can cause depressed fracture of the skull and other injuries resulting in death, and leave no visible evidence whatsoever.

The peculiar vesicular or bulbous eruptions characteristic of smallpox would remain if the disease proved fatal. Bubonic plague and Hodgkin's disease would show signs of enlarged glands in the groin, and enlarged glands could also result from some forms of tuberculosis. Certain forms of osteogenic sarcoma and bone tuberculosis would give rise to tumours externally visible. Some pathological changes caused by the spirocheate *Treponema pallida* could leave external signs, but Ruffer states that no case of syphilis has been observed in ancient Egyptian skeletal material. Leprosy too may leave visible evidence, but death in this case is usually brought about by other causes.

The above list virtually exhausts the various causes of death that give rise to enduring external signs.[1] It is hardly surprising therefore, in view of the infinite number of other diseases and possible causes, that Derry, with only the results of an anatomical examination to help him, was unable to furnish this highly desirable information.

[1] Cf., in general, M. A. Ruffer, *Studies in the Palaeopathology of Egypt* (Chicago, 1921); G. Elliot Smith and W. R. Dawson, *Egyptian Mummies* (London, 1924), pp. 154–62; W. R. Dawson, *Magician and Leech* (London, 1929), pp. 103–8; H. E. Sigerist, *A History of Medicine*, I (New York, 1941), pp. 37–101; J. T. Rowling, *Proc. Royal Soc. of Medicine*, 54 (1961), pp. 409–15. [Ed.]

It must also be remembered that the various operative procedures involved in mummification and the alteration of the soft tissues caused by the process, together with the peculiar and unusual carbonization of parts of the body, as described by both Carter and Derry, and the manipulations necessitated by the adhesion of the body to the gold coffin, combine to further obscure any signs that might indicate the cause of death.

THE OTHER HUMAN REMAINS

IN a plain wooden box found in the Treasury were two miniature anthropoid coffins of gilded wood, each one containing another similar coffin, within which was a mummified foetus.[1] The brief inscriptions on the four coffins are without names, and thus provide no clue as to the identity of the remains.

Carter's card catalogue includes the report of their examination by Derry. This constitutes all that is known about the two foetuses, since no further reference whatsoever is to be found in any of Carter's notes or Derry's surviving manuscripts. There is no clue as to the date of the examination, which cannot, however, have taken place at the same time as that of the pharaoh, since work on the Treasury did not begin until after that in the Burial Chamber had been completed.

Nor do any of Carter's notes give an indication as to their whereabouts, although it might be assumed that they were transferred to the Cairo Museum. Carter himself kept a record of the contents of boxes prepared for dispatch to the Museum. Full details are given of the consignments sent on 11 April 1927, and in March 1929, but only one page remains of an undated consignment between, the rest having been removed from the diary. On this surviving page, among a number of other entries, mention is made of, 'Case XXXIII. Two miniature coffins Nos. 317 *a*, 317 *b*', which may have been meant to include the inner coffins and foetuses, though nothing is said about these.

The information contained in Carter's card catalogue is as follows. The transcription of Derry's notes on the examination of the two foetuses has been verified from a draft included among the manuscripts held by Professor Emery.

317 *a* (2). A MINIATURE MUMMY ritualistically wrapped. Head covered with a gesso-gilt mask, several sizes too large.

Wrapping: linen covering; five transverse bands; two triple longitudinal bands around sides and over front and back, in the sense of a normal mummy of the period. The wrappings comprised about 1·5 cm. in thickness, but were in bad order: pads over chest, legs and stiffeners for feet were very apparent.

Contents: a child of premature birth, perfectly preserved.

317 *a* (2). [Plate XXIV, left] MUMMY OF A CHILD: examination by Derry.

This is the body of a prematurely-born child, probably female. The length from the vertex of the head to the heels [is] 25·75 cm.

The body had been carefully wrapped in linen, but this had already been removed.[2] There is no abdominal incision and no indication as to how the body was preserved.

The skin is of a greyish colour, very shrunken and brittle, and the clavicles, ribs and costal cartilages are all plainly seen through it. On the limbs it has become pressed into folds owing to the loss by dessication of the natural fullness produced by the underlying tissues, and here also the bones of the hands are clearly defined.

The limbs are fully extended, and the hands are resting on the front of the thighs.

[1] Cf. Plate XXIII.
[2] Carter here interpolates: 'I had unwrapped this mummy before Derry saw it—the wrapping had been carried out in the XVIIIth dynasty method.'

There is no sign of either eyebrows or eyelashes. The eyelids are nearly closed and the small aperture between the lids which now exists is almost certainly a secondary result due to retraction of the lids owing to shrinkage of the parts in drying.

On the head are visible many fine whitish hairs of a silky appearance, probably the remains of lanugo.

A portion of the umbilical cord is present and measures 21 mm. in length. The umbilicus is still at a low level.

Allowing for general shrinkage of the body, it is estimated from the length of the foetus, the absence of eyebrows and eyelashes and the state of the eyelids, that the intra-uterine age of the child when born could not have exceeded five months.

317 *b* (2). A MINIATURE MUMMY ritualistically wrapped. Length 39·5 cm. overall.

System of wrapping layers: (1) A triple longitudinal band over front and back; a triple longitudinal band round sides; three triple transverse bands, round neck, abdomen, and ankles, and one double, round head.   (2) Under which a linen covering.   (3) Under covering sheet, transverse wrapping, and a plaited band round edge of toes.   (4) A folded sheet over the whole of the front.   (5) Transverse and criss-cross bandaging; large stiffening pads over feet, for strength and shape.   (6) Large side pads with bandages to hold them in place.   (7) Broad bands wound round transversely.   (8) Large folds of linen (pads) to make good the legs.   (9) Transverse bandages holding thick pads over abdomen and chest.   (10) Numerous transverse bandages; large shapen pad to make up feet.   (11) Thin strips of linen wound round transversely some twenty-four times to hold undercovering sheets and pads in place.   (12) Large covering sheets wound transversely and much charred.   (13) Some finer linen coverings over the actual flesh.

Contents: mummy of an infant (?) of normal birth. Length 37·7 cm. Preservation not so good as 317 *a* (2).

317 *b* (2). [Plate XXIV, right] MUMMY OF A CHILD: examination by Derry.

This child, probably a girl, whose length from vertex to heels is 36·1 cm., is also of premature birth.

The skin is of much the same colour and in the same condition as that of the younger foetus. The linen wrappings which are in a very friable state are still partially attached to the child.

The limbs are fully extended, but in this case the hands are placed beside the thighs in the position of pronation.

The scalp is free from hair except for some very fine downy-looking hairs in the occipital region, but most of the hair has probably come away with the bandages. The eyebrows are distinct and a few eyelashes remain.

The eyes are wide open and the orbital cavity contains only the shrunken eyeball with no packing.

On opening the head through the anterior fontanelle the cranial cavity was found filled with linen apparently impregnated with some saline material. The linen had been inserted through the nose. A wire passed through the right nostril appeared in the cranial cavity as seen through the fontanelle.

There is no sign of the umbilical cord but the appearance of the navel which is not retracted suggests that the cord had been removed by cutting it off close to the abdominal wall and that it had not dried up as it would had the child lived.

The abdominal wall has been opened by an incision 18 mm. in length on the left side, immediately above the inguinal ligament and parallel with it. The opening was closed with a sealing of resin.[1] The abdominal cavity is stuffed with linen impregnated with some saline material.

The nails appear to be fully grown, but allowing for the shrinkage of the soft tissues it is possible that they were not fully developed.

The maximum length of the head is 84·0 mm. and the width 73·0 mm.

The length of the foetus and its apparent development would make it to have been about seven months at the time of birth.

ANALYSES: A. Lucas.

No. 317 *b* (2).

Cranial Cavity: This consists of disintegrated woven fabric (probably linen) impregnated and covered with minute crystals of common salt. There is no evidence of resin.

Abdomen: Practically identical with the material from the cranial cavity. The white crystals are common salt. There is no evidence of resin.

Material covering Incision in Abdomen: This gives negative tests for resin and for beeswax. It gives very definite positive tests for nitrogenous organic matter (i.e. animal matter). It is suggested that it consists of altered animal tissue.

In a large percentage of cases it is quite impossible even at the time, to diagnose the cause of still birth and foetal death, and after mummification any sign or symptom that might be present would be made even more obscure. Nevertheless, it was felt that if an examination of the two foetuses could be made, more knowledge than is at present available might result, though it was clearly too much to hope that the cause of death would be revealed, or possible indications of parentage be obtained.

The Egyptian Department of Antiquities kindly gave permission for an anatomical and X-ray examination of the two bodies, but when, in January 1971, the time came to make the examination, the whereabouts of the remains could not be established. The glass case in the Tutʿankhamūn gallery in the Cairo Museum was opened, and the small anthropoid coffins were found to be empty. With the help of Dr. Riad a search was made of other likely containers, but without success, and neither were the foetuses to be found in the Museum's two magazines.

In the index of the Museum's Temporary Journal, the coffins were seen to have been recorded under three different headings, but there was no mention of the foetuses. Nor was there any reference to them in the *Journal d'Entrée*.

As hope of finding them in the Museum receded, it was thought that they might have been retained in Derry's collection of specimens held in the Kasr El-Ainy Hospital. Examination of that portion of the collection retained in the Anatomy School, and partial examination of the remainder now housed in the basement of the hospital, proved equally unsuccessful.

---

[1] But see Lucas's analysis.

APPENDIX 1

OUR knowledge of the length and position of the abdominal incision made by the royal embalmers during the process of mummification is gained chiefly from the work of Elliot Smith.[1] In his *Royal Mummies* he emphasizes the fact that the position of the incision varied with different practitioners. The two positions shown in Fig. 1*a* were frequently used, while a third, Fig. 1*b* was occasionally employed.

The atypical site of the incision made in the case of Tutʿankhamūn is seen in Fig. 1*c*. The line here chosen by the royal embalmer is one not noted by Elliot Smith.

Derry records that the length of the abdominal incision appeared to be 86 mm., but comments that the overlying resin may have obscured the original extent. This is feasible, since many incisions were as much as half as long again.

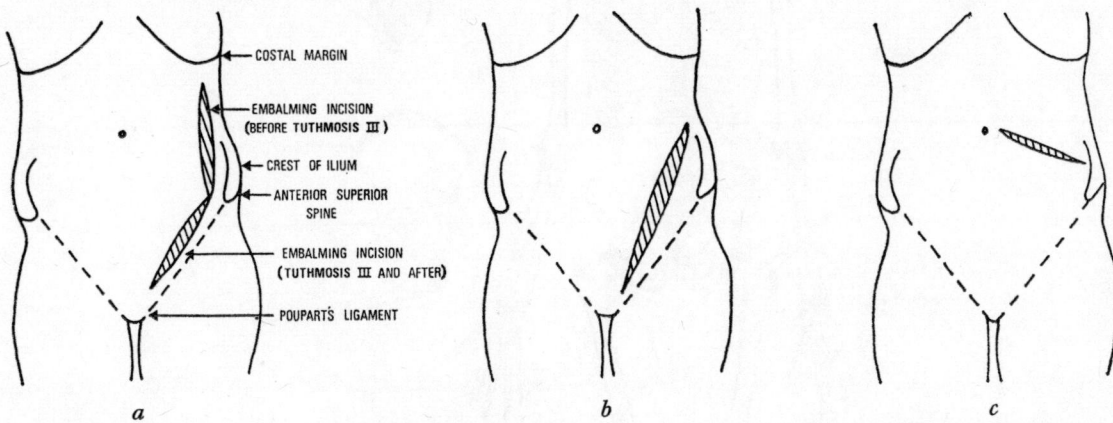

Fig. 1

---

[1] Cf., in general, K. Sudhoff, *Archiv für Geschichte der Medizin*, 5 (1911), pp. 161–71; W. R. Dawson, *Proc. Royal Soc. of Medicine*, 20 (1927), pp. 843–4; *JEA*, 13 (1927), pp. 42–3. [Ed.]

APPENDIX 2

As an indication of the approximate ages between which the epiphyseal ends become fully calcified and unite, Fig. 2 illustrates the range most generally accepted. These figures refer, however, to Europeans, and it is recognized that among Eastern peoples maturation tends to take place earlier.[1]

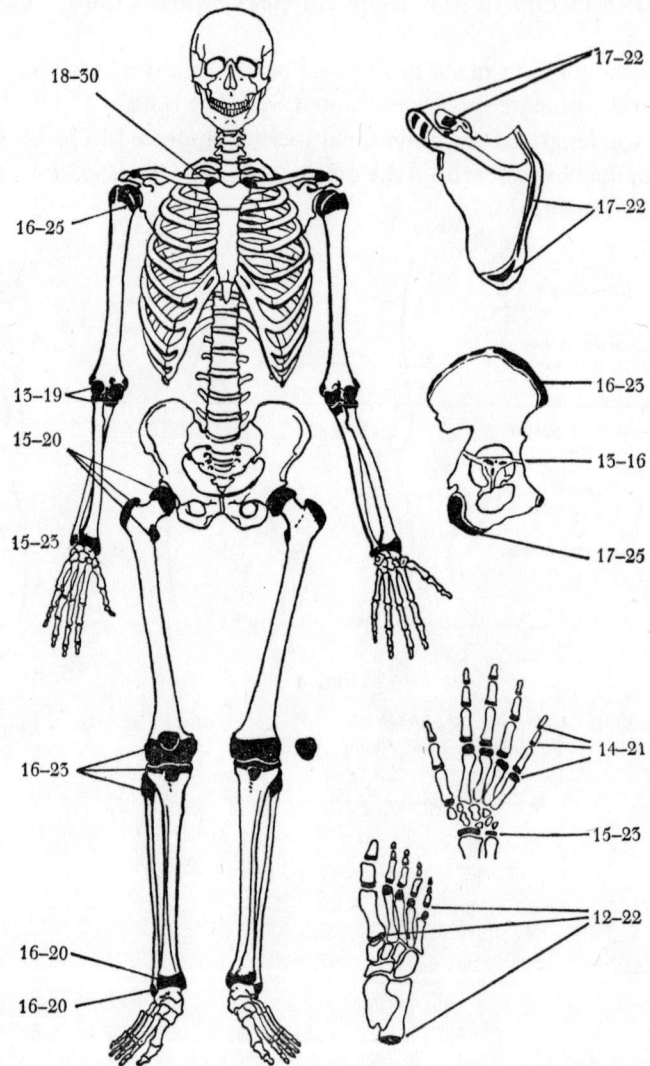

Fig. 2

---

[1] Cf. the reassessment of such evidence in the case of the human remains now thought to be those of Smenkhkareʿ: R. G. Harrison, *JEA*, 52 (1966), pp. 95–119. [Ed.]

NOTES TO THE PLATES

Plate I. Dr. Douglas E. Derry begins the examination of the Royal Mummy by making the first incision into the outermost wrappings. Grouped round the coffin, from left to right, are: Pierre Lacau, Director of the Department of Antiquities; Howard Carter (with glass); Tewfik Effendi Boulos, Chief Inspector, Department of Antiquities, Upper Egypt (partly hidden); H.E. Sayed Fuad Bey el Kholi, Governor of the Province of Qena; Alfred Lucas, Government Chemist and honorary consulting chemist to the Department of Antiquities; H.E. Saleh Enan Pasha, Under-Secretary of State to the Ministry of Public Works (leaning forward); his secretary; Dr. D. E. Derry; Dr. Saleh Bey Hamdi.

GI neg. 939.

Photograph by Harry Burton. Griffith Institute.

Plate II. The Royal Mummy: the outermost wrappings, and those revealed beneath. The external appearance of the mummy belies the fragility and decay of the linen wrappings, the condition of which became clear when the outer layers were removed.

(left) GI neg. 780A = MMA neg. TAA 513.
(right) GI neg. 1596.

Photographs by Harry Burton. Griffith Institute.

Plate III. The Royal Mummy: two further stages in the unwrapping, showing successive layers of amulets and insignia placed in the bandages.

(left) GI neg. 1567 = MMA neg. TAA 1252.
(right) GI neg. 780 = MMA neg. TAA 516.

Photographs by Harry Burton. Griffith Institute.

Plate IV. The Royal Mummy: the last stages in the exposure of the lower limbs, showing further items of jewellery and revealing the cracked condition of the soft tissue.

(left) GI neg. 783 = MMA neg. TAA 1249.
(right) GI neg. 783A = MMA neg. TAA 518.

Photographs by Harry Burton. Griffith Institute.

Plate V. The Royal Mummy: four stages in the unwrapping of the head, showing the rope-like 'lawaya' (top left), the inlaid gold diadem (top right, bottom left), the outer gold head-band (bottom left), and the gold uraeus and vulture crowning the brow (bottom right).

(top left) GI neg. 792A = MMA neg. TAA 1248.
(top right) GI neg. 1575 = MMA neg. TAA 1247.
(bottom left) GI neg. 805 = MMA neg. TAA 528.
(bottom right) GI neg. 806 = MMA neg. TAA 527.

Photographs by Harry Burton. Griffith Institute.

Plate VI. The Royal Mummy: front and left profile views of the head at the final stage of unwrapping, showing the second, inner gold head-band and part of the beadwork skull-cap.

(left) GI neg. 808 = MMA neg. TAA 1153.
(right) GI neg. 809 = MMA neg. TAA 535.

Photographs by Harry Burton. Griffith Institute.

Plates VII, VIII, IX. The Royal Mummy: right profile and side views of the head; three-quarter views of the head from left and right; left side and profile views of the head. The last wrappings have been removed and only the beaded skull-cap remains in place. Apart from the surface cracks in the skin and the flattening of the cartilaginous part of the nose by the bandaging, the head has deteriorated less than the rest of the body. The lashes are well preserved on the right eye, the large incisor teeth show clearly between the lips, and the perforation made for a ring or plug is still visible in the lobe of the left ear. The lobe of the right ear appears to have been detached along with the bandages, while the top of the left ear was broken away in removing the inner gold head-band (cf. Plate VI). In front of this ear is a rounded depression suggesting a scab. For a view of the head as it now is, cf. *JEA*, 57 (1971), pl. 29.

(VII left) GI neg. 810 = MMA neg. TAA 532.

(VII right) GI neg. 1594.

(VIII left) GI neg. 1578 = MMA neg. TAA 530.

(VIII right) GI neg. 815.

(IX left) GI neg. 1510 = MMA neg. TAA 533.

(IX right) GI neg. 1577 = MMA neg. TAA 1244.

Photographs by Harry Burton. Griffith Institute.

Plate X, top. The Royal Mummy: back view of the head, with the skull-cap in place.

GI neg. 812 = MMA neg. TAA 531.

Photograph by Harry Burton. Griffith Institute.

Plate X, bottom. The Royal Mummy: the pad of linen from upon the head, composed of wads and bandages in a good state of preservation.

GI neg. 1595 = MMA neg. TAA 1240.

Photograph by Harry Burton. Griffith Institute.

Plate XI. The Royal Mummy: top view of the head, with the skull-cap in place. The cartouches within the uraei contain the didactic name of the Aten in a hitherto unrecorded variant.

GI neg. 812A = MMA neg. TAA 529.

Photograph by Harry Burton. Griffith Institute.

Plate XII. The Royal Mummy: the severed trunk after it had been cut through above the iliac crests, and with the head detached (cf. Plate XXI).

GI neg. 785.

Photograph by Harry Burton. Griffith Institute.

Plates XIII, XIV, XV. The Royal Mummy: the abdomen and lower limbs; detail of the lower abdomen and upper parts of the legs; detail of the lower parts of the legs. The shrunken and cracked condition of the soft tissue coverage is revealed in detail, some cracks having coalesced and penetrated as far as the bone so that parts have disintegrated. The embalming incision is visible on the left side of the lower abdomen.

(XIII) GI neg. 786 = MMA neg. TAA 517.

(XIV) GI neg. 817 = MMA neg. TAA 1133.

(XV) GI neg. 1583 = MMA neg. TAA 520.

Photographs by Harry Burton. Griffith Institute.

Plates XVI, XVII. The Royal Mummy: the right hand and forearm; the right hand and forearm disarticulated. The flexed, prehensile attitude is the result of bandaging, the removal of which has destroyed the soft tissue covering the metacarpal bones and detached the thumb. The gold finger-stalls remain in position. The wrist has been disarticulated through the epiphyseal line of the radius and the lower end of the ulna.

(XVI) GI neg. 1576 = MMA neg. TAA 540.

(XVII) GI neg. 1580 = MMA neg. TAA 1243.

Photographs by Harry Burton. Griffith Institute.

Plate XVIII. The Royal Mummy: parts of the scapulae, and the heads of the humeri.

    A: part of the anterior aspect of the right scapula (1-coracoid process; 2-acromion; 3-glenoid cavity).

    B: part of the anterior aspect of the left scapula (1–3 as above).

    C: the heads of the humeri; much of the outer compact bone is missing, revealing the inner cancellous tissue.

GI neg. 1579 = MMA neg. TAA 1242.

Photograph by Harry Burton. Griffith Institute.

Plate XIX. The Royal Mummy: the feet, with the gold sandals and toe-stalls still in position. When the sandals were removed, some of the cracked soft tissue disintegrated.

GI neg. 1556 = MMA neg. TAA 1241.

Photograph by Harry Burton. Griffith Institute.

Plate XX. The Royal Mummy: the body unwrapped and reassembled upon a tray of sand, before the last stages of the examination. The thorax and forearms still retain some of their bandages.

GI neg. 1566 = MMA neg. TAA 539.

Photograph by Harry Burton. Griffith Institute.

Plate XXI. The Royal Mummy: lateral X-ray of the head, showing the two (opaque) areas of resin poured into the back and top of the cranial cavity through a hole in the cribriform plate of the ethmoid bone (not visible in this projection). Because of the superposition of structures, most of the details of the teeth are also obscured, but on the original radiograph it was possible to discern that the apices of the lower right third molar are open and not fully formed, and it is therefore probable that the minimum estimate of the king's age at death is the more correct (cf. pp. 7, 13, 17).

X-ray by Professor R. G. Harrison.

Photograph by courtesy of The Times.

Plate XXII. The Royal Mummy: X-ray of the trunk, showing the line of the cut made through it above the iliac crests. The tiny rings scattered on either side of the cervical vertebrae are small beads that still adhere to the body.

X-ray by Professor R. G. Harrison.

Photograph by courtesy of The Times.

[The quality of the two reproductions could not be improved without the use of the original radiographs, and these were not made available.]

Plate XXIII. The mummies of the two foetuses in their respective coffins—on the left the smaller one (317 a), and on the right the larger (317 b).

(left) GI neg. 1064.

(right) GI neg. 1061.

Photographs by Harry Burton. Griffith Institute.

Plate XXIV. The two foetuses after unwrapping. The bodies are those of prematurely born children, probably female, the estimated intra-uterine age of the smaller (317 a [2]) being not more than five months, and of the larger (317 b [2]) about seven months. In the case of the latter, some of the packing within the cranial cavity is visible through the anterior fontanelle.

(left) GI neg. 1063 = MMA neg. TAA 382.

(right) GI neg. 1062 = MMA neg. TAA 385.

Photographs by Harry Burton. Griffith Institute.

Fig. 1 (p. 25). Line drawing by Clive F. Ahrens, *a–b* after G. Elliot Smith, *The Royal Mummies*, Cairo 1912.

Fig. 2 (p. 26). Line drawing reproduced from D. R. Brothwell, *Digging up Bones*, London 1963—by courtesy of the Trustees of the British Museum.

PLATE I

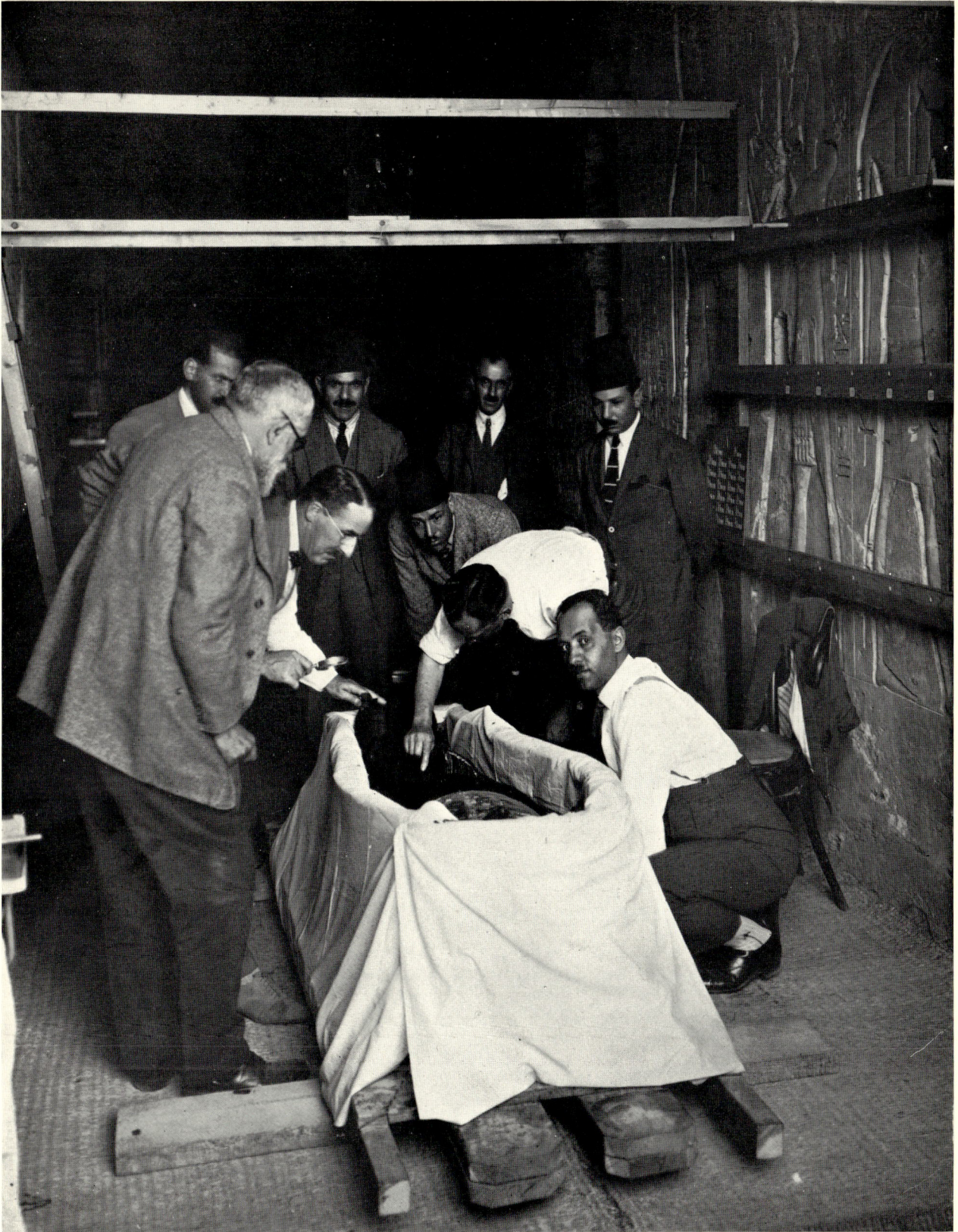

Dr. Douglas E. Derry begins the examination of the Royal Mummy
Photograph by Harry Burton. Griffith Institute

PLATE II

The Royal Mummy: the outermost wrappings, and those revealed beneath
Photographs by Harry Burton. Griffith Institute

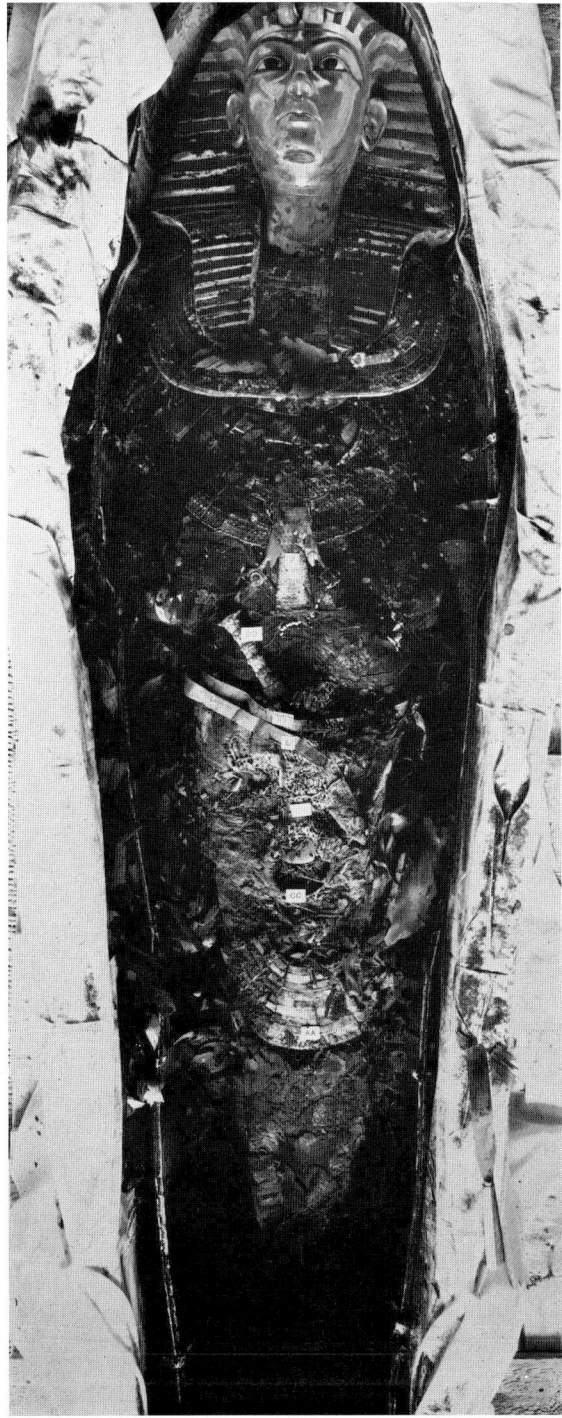

PLATE III

The Royal Mummy: two further stages in the unwrapping

Photographs by Harry Burton. Griffith Institute

PLATE IV

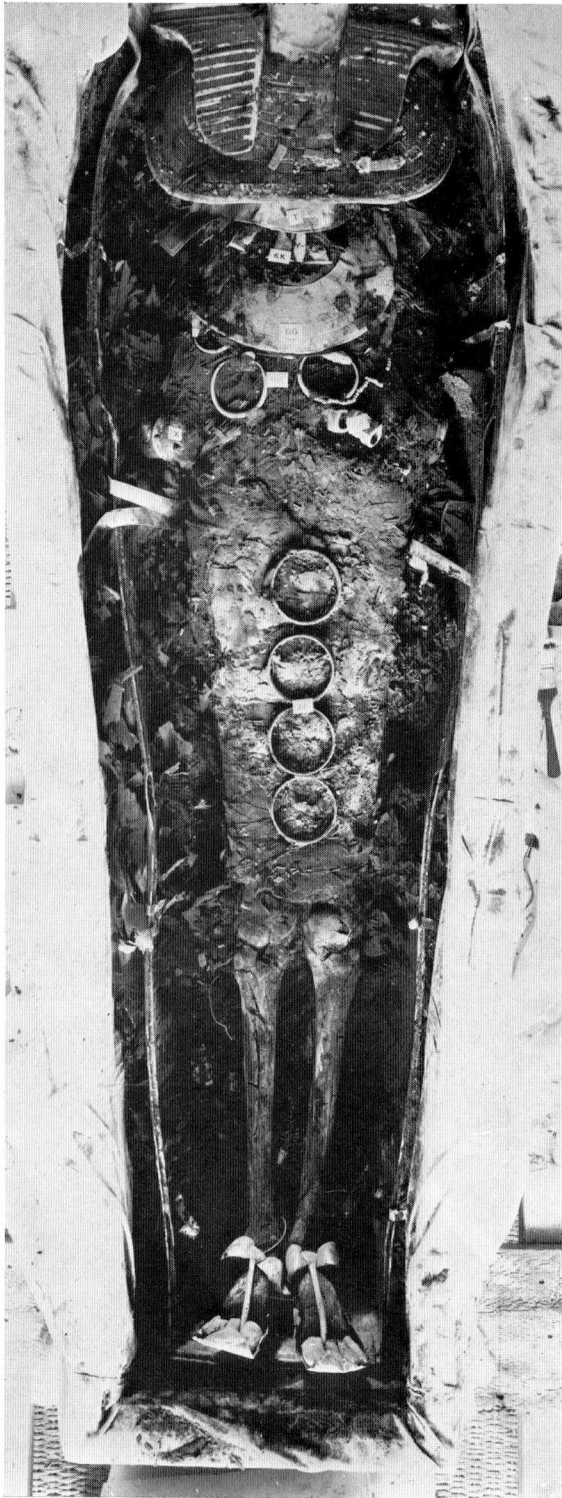

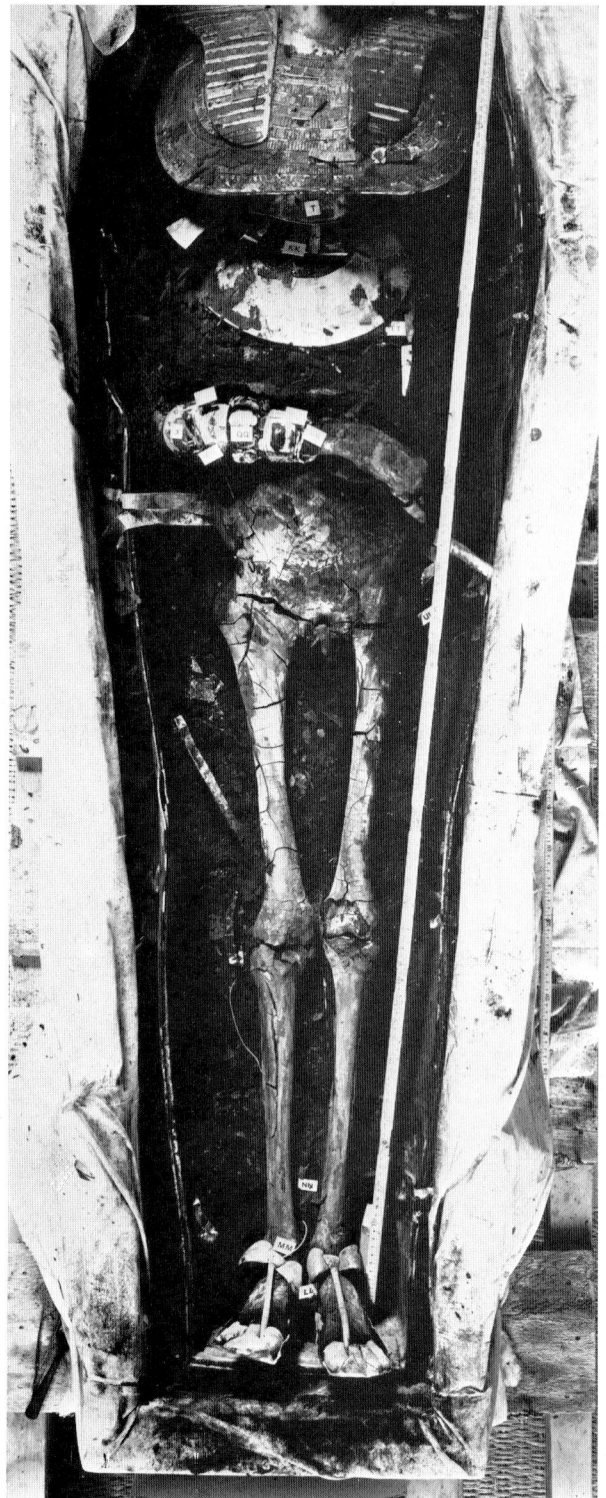

The Royal Mummy: the last stages in the exposure of the lower limbs
Photographs by Harry Burton. Griffith Institute

PLATE V

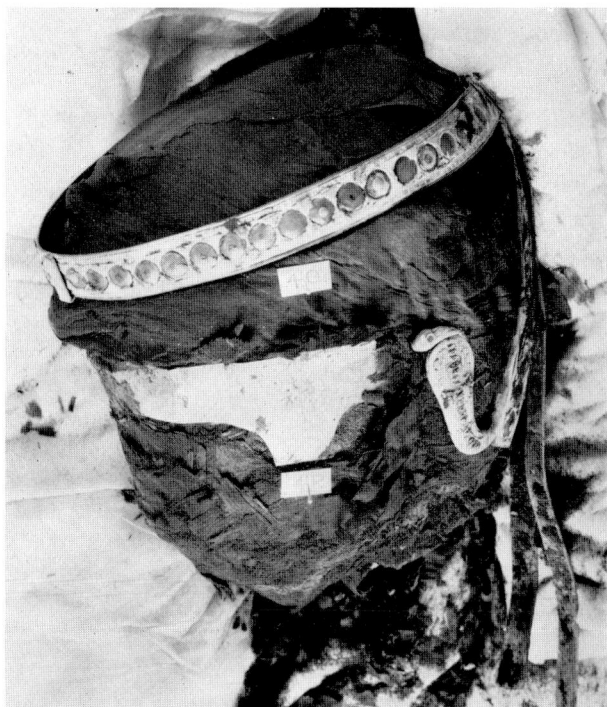

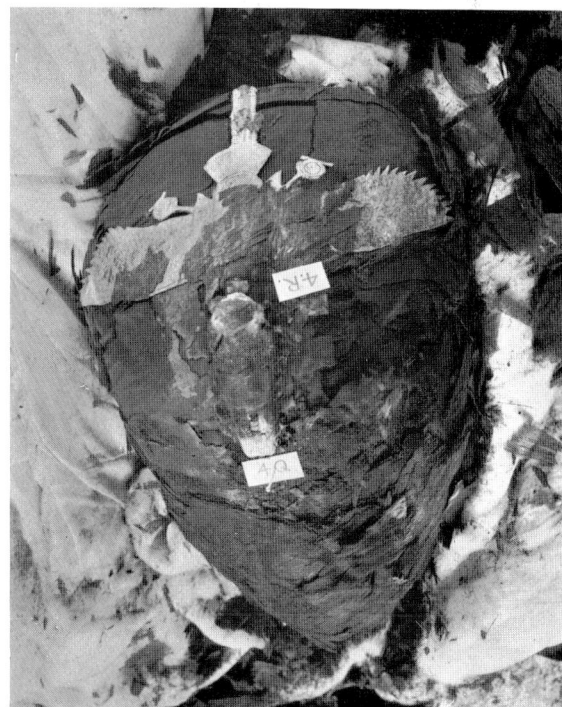

The Royal Mummy: four stages in the unwrapping of the head
Photographs by Harry Burton. Griffith Institute

PLATE VI

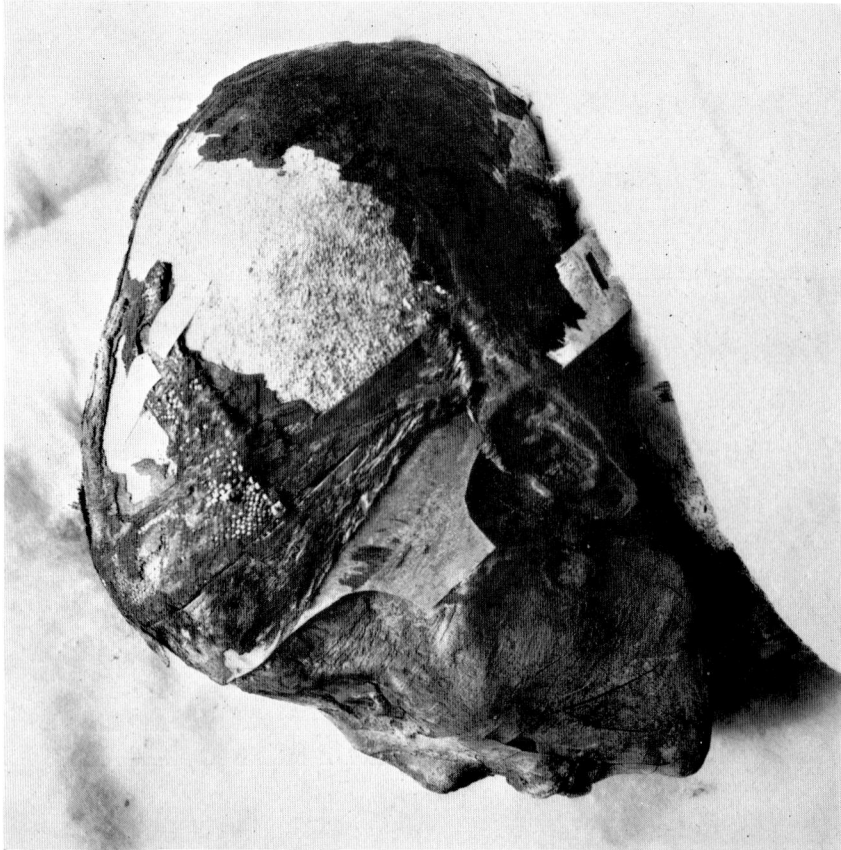

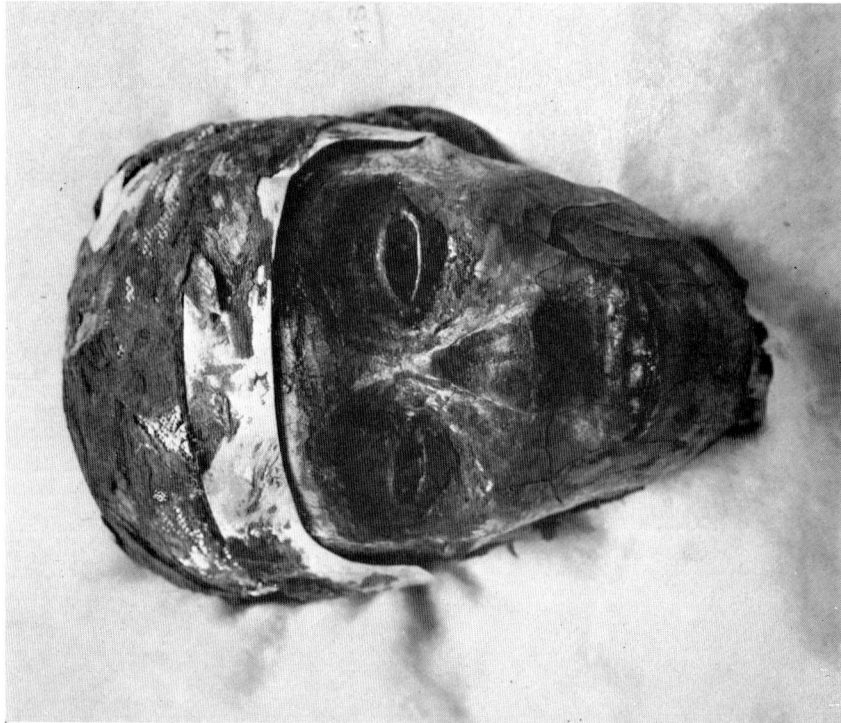

The Royal Mummy: front and left profile views of the head at the final stage of unwrapping
Photographs by Harry Burton. Griffith Institute

PLATE VII

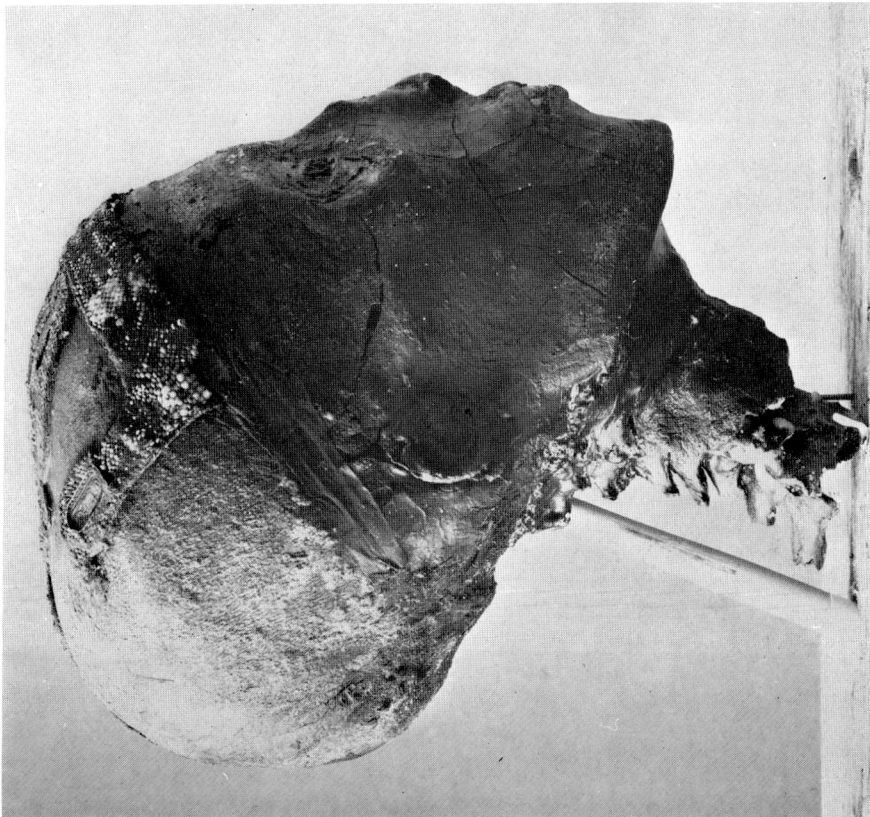

The Royal Mummy: right profile and side views of the head
Photographs by Harry Burton. Griffith Institute

PLATE VIII

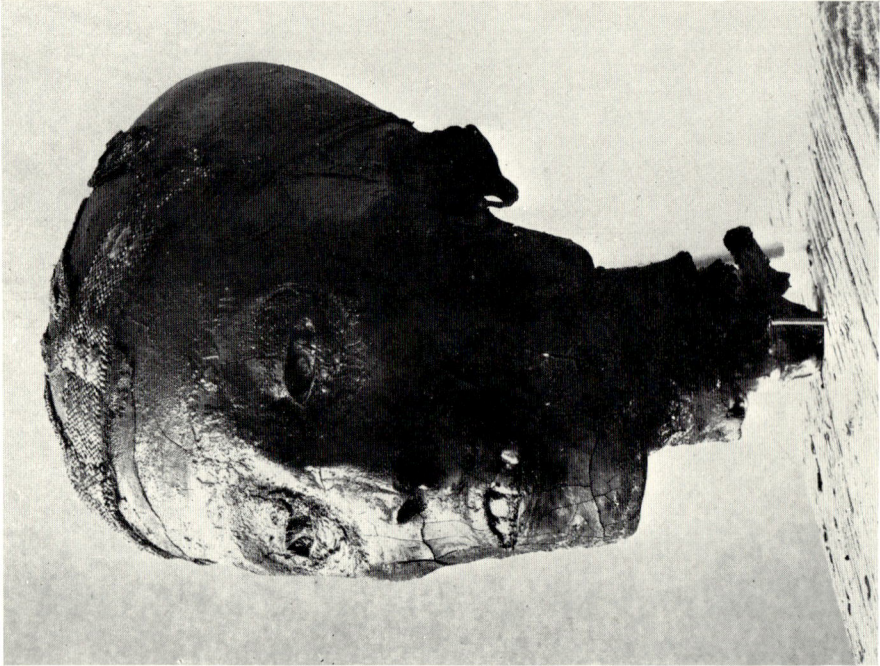

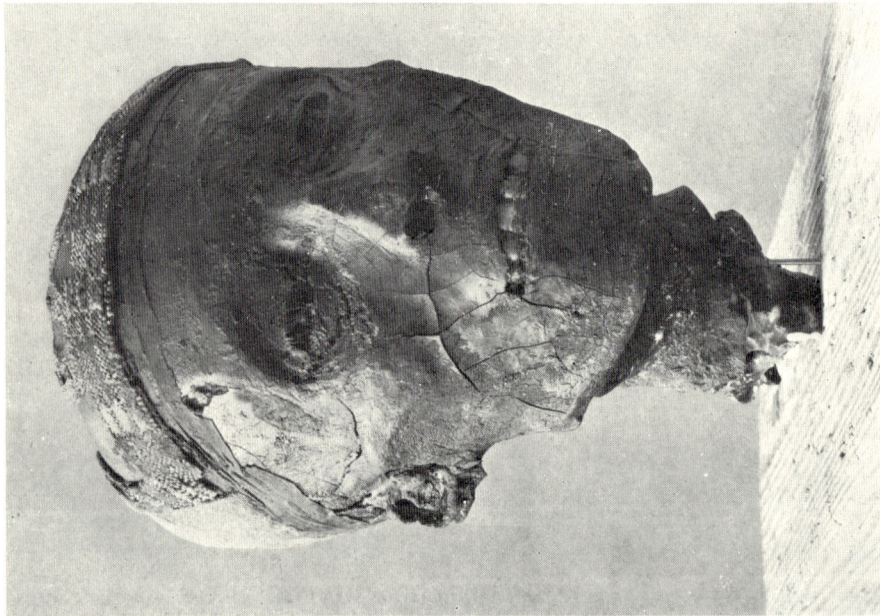

The Royal Mummy: three-quarter views of the head from left and right

Photographs by Harry Burton. Griffith Institute

PLATE IX

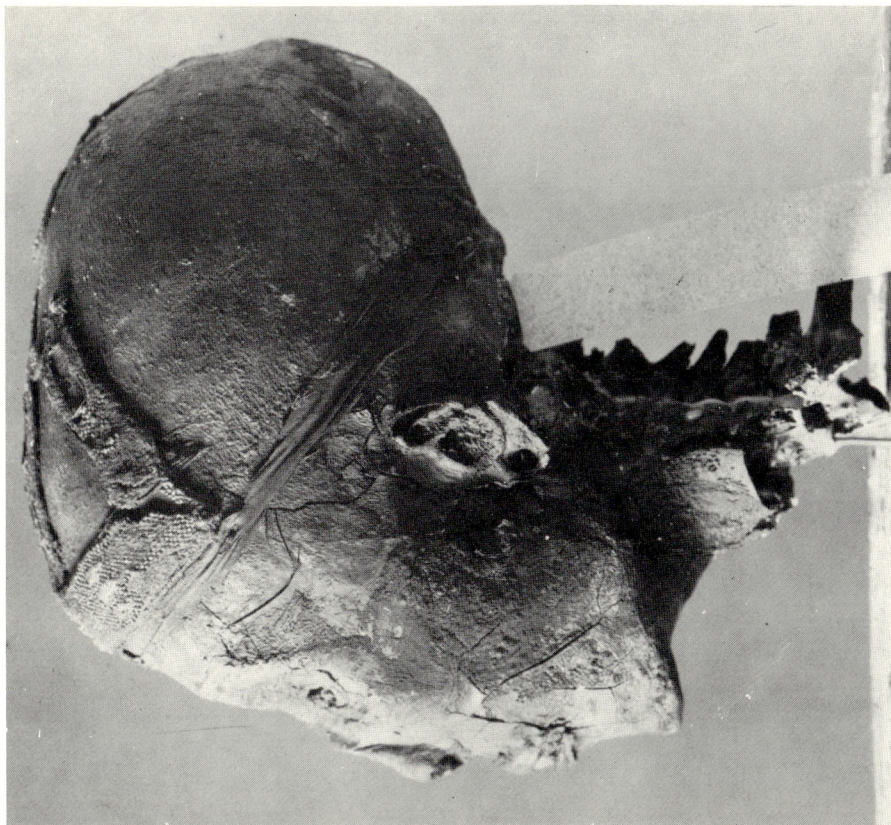

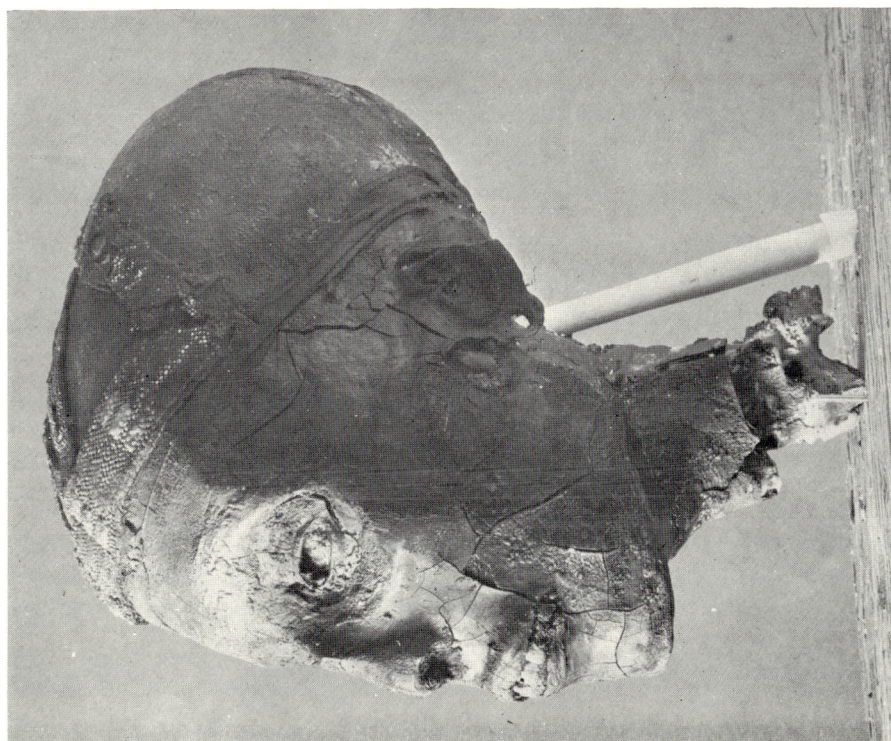

The Royal Mummy: left side and profile views of the head
Photographs by Harry Burton. Griffith Institute

PLATE X

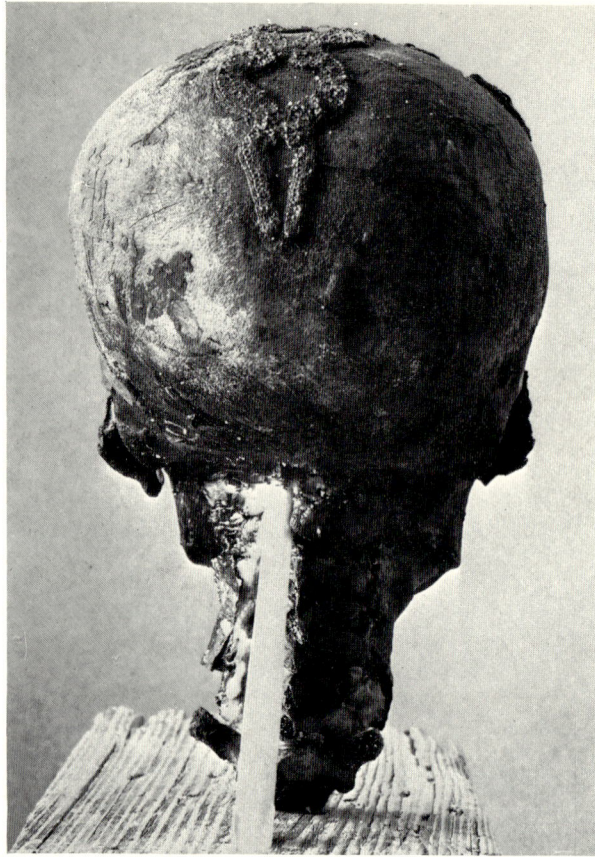

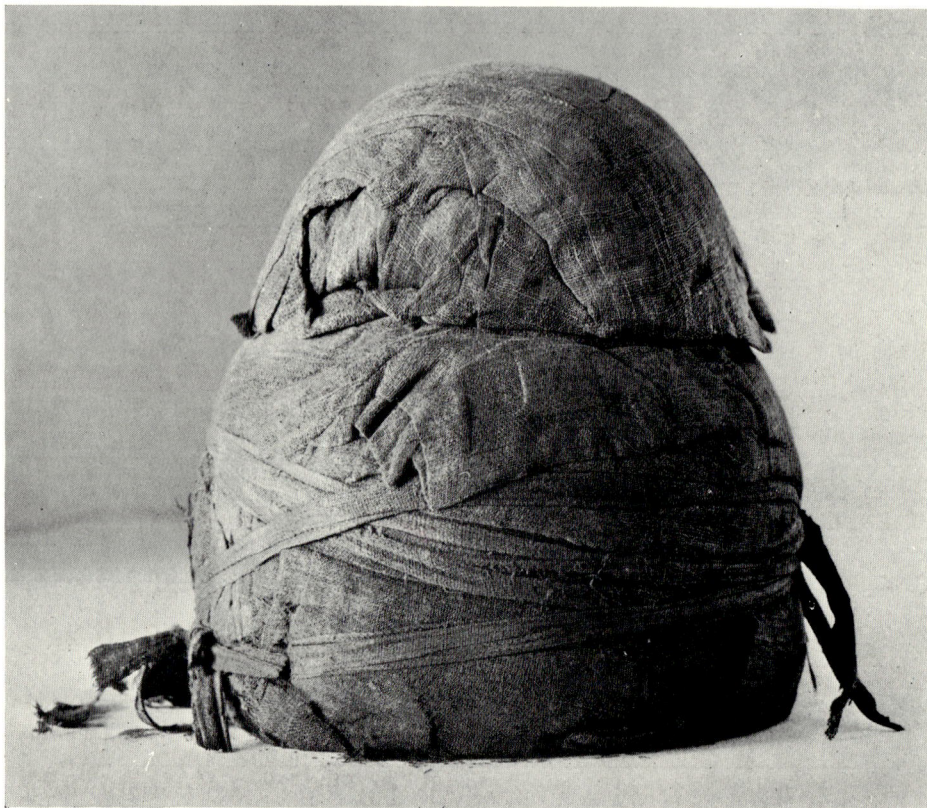

The Royal Mummy: back view of the head, and the pad of linen from upon it

Photographs by Harry Burton Griffith Institute

PLATE XI

The Royal Mummy: top view of the head
Photograph by Harry Burton. Griffith Institute

PLATE XII

The Royal Mummy: the severed trunk
Photograph by Harry Burton. Griffith Institute

PLATE XIII

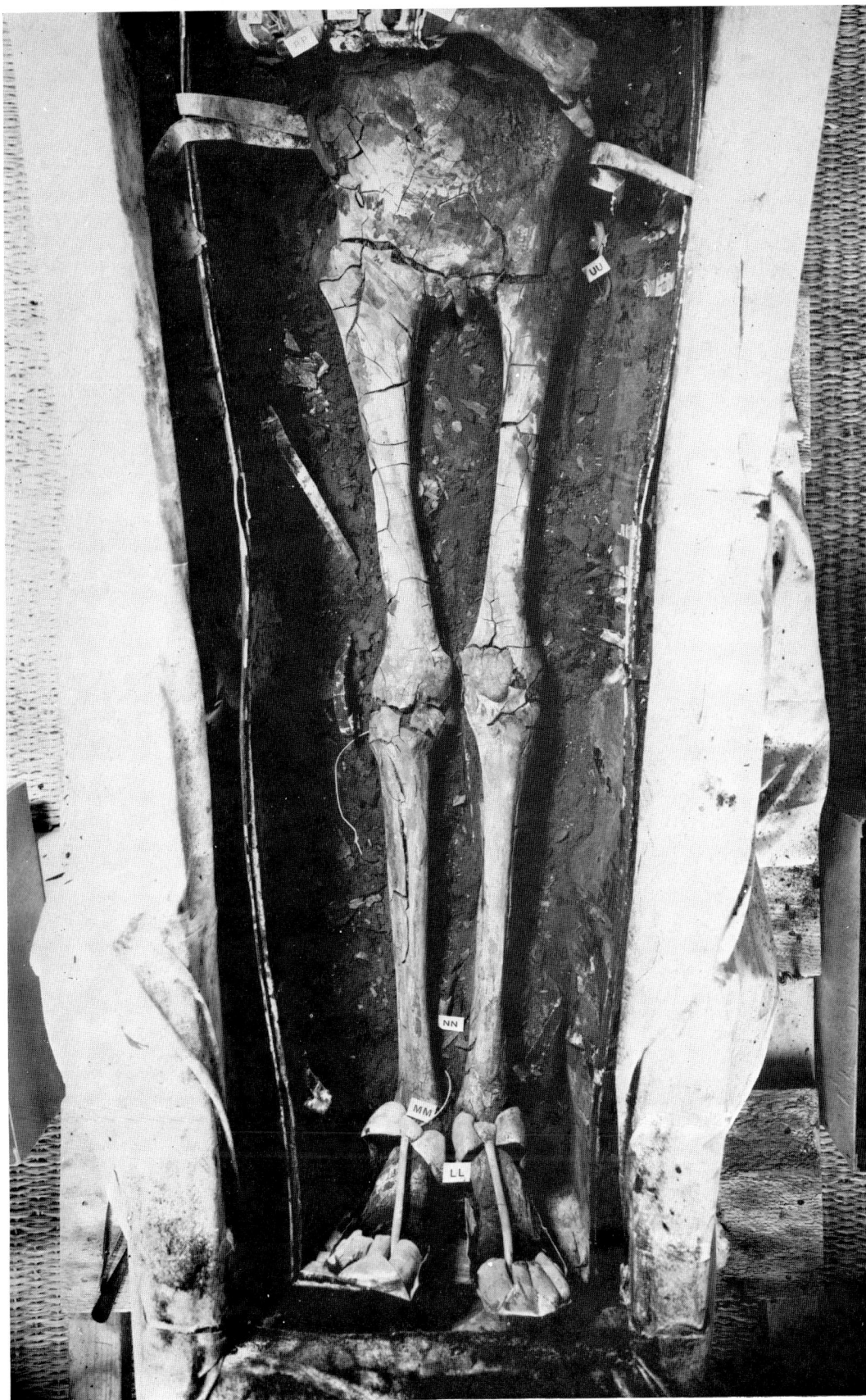

The Royal Mummy: the abdomen and lower limbs
Photograph by Harry Burton. Griffith Institute

PLATE XIV

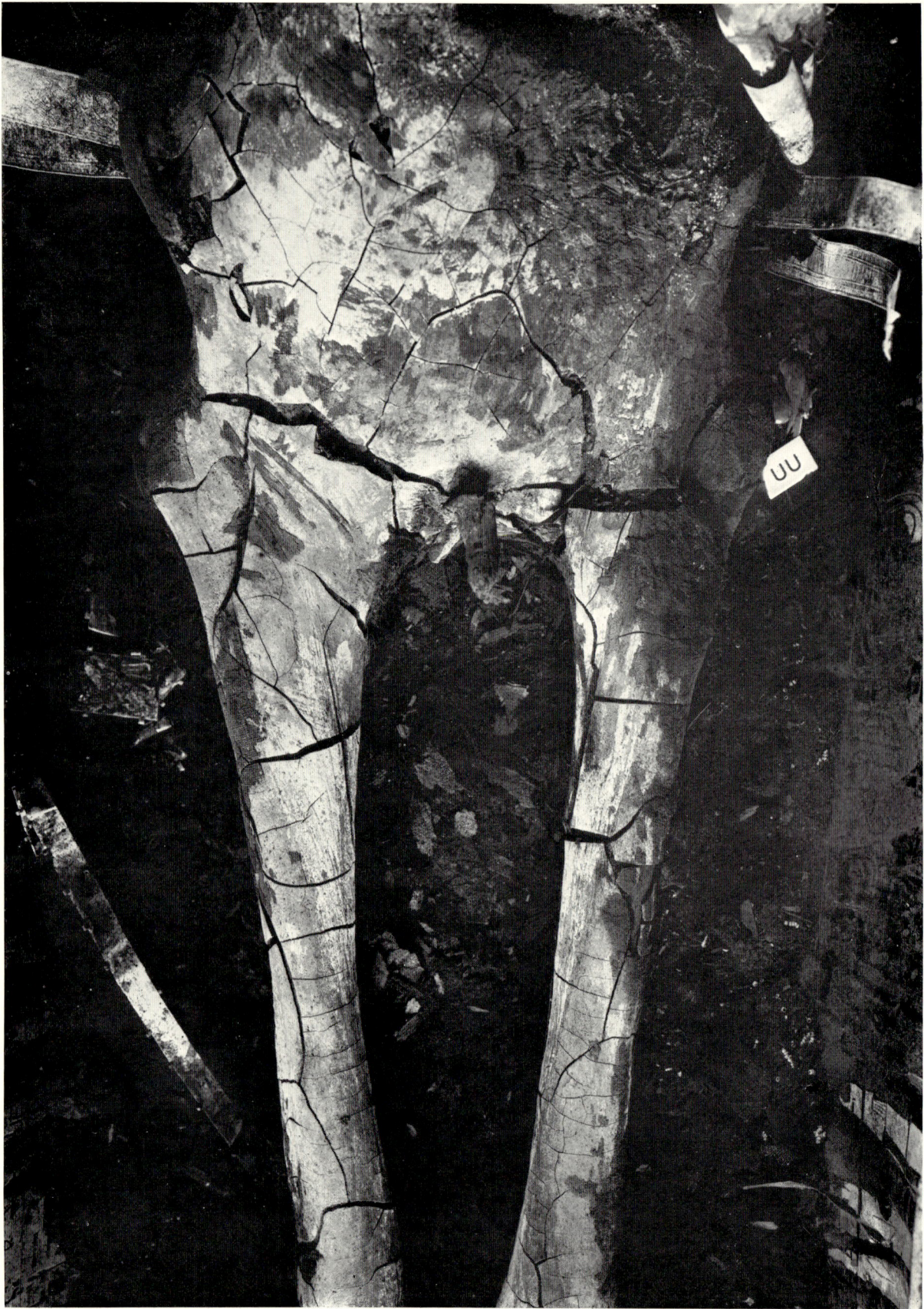

The Royal Mummy: detail of the lower abdomen and upper parts of the legs
Photograph by Harry Burton. Griffith Institute

PLATE XV

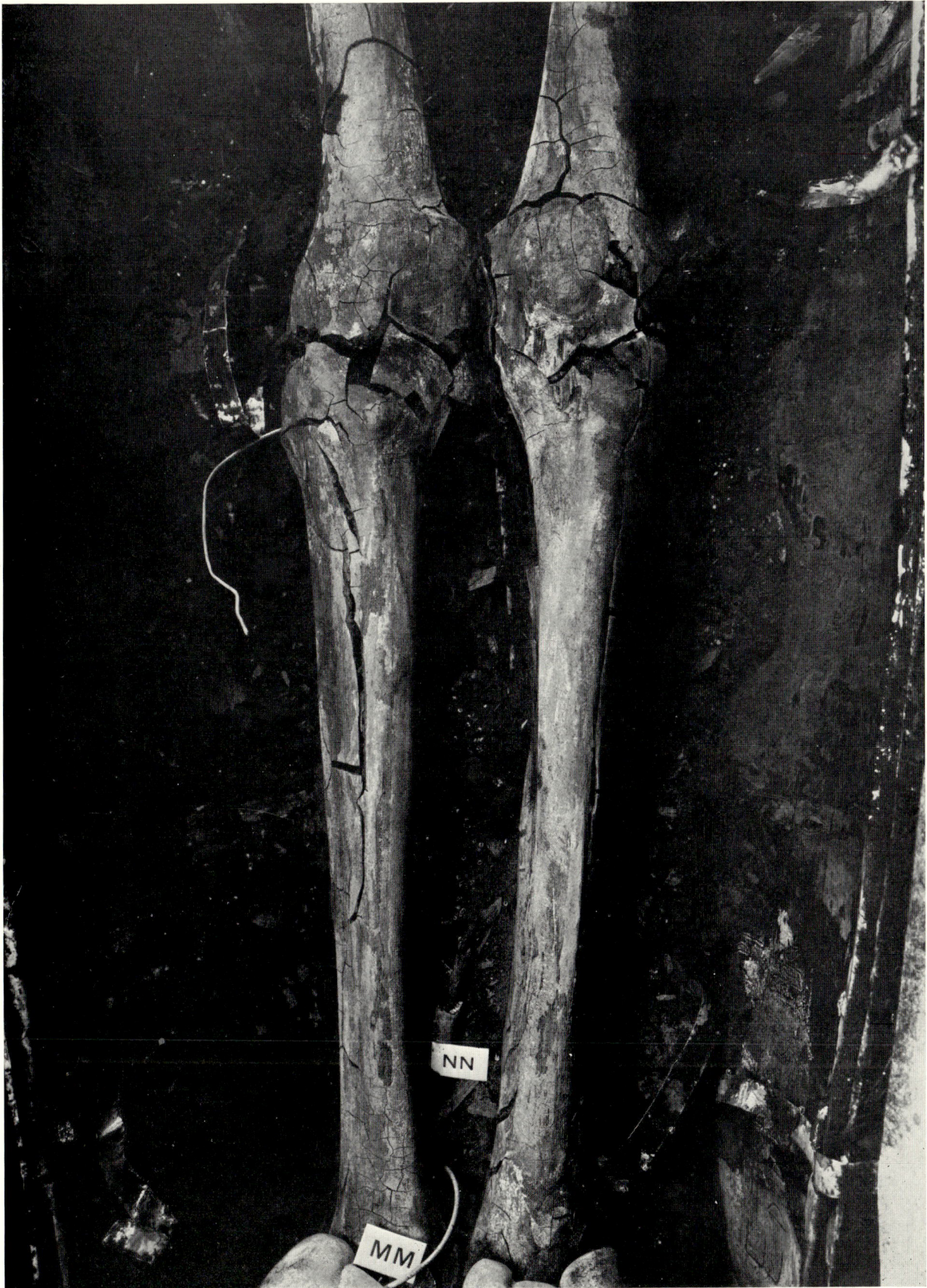

The Royal Mummy: detail of the lower parts of the legs

Photograph by Harry Burton. Griffith Institute

PLATE XVI

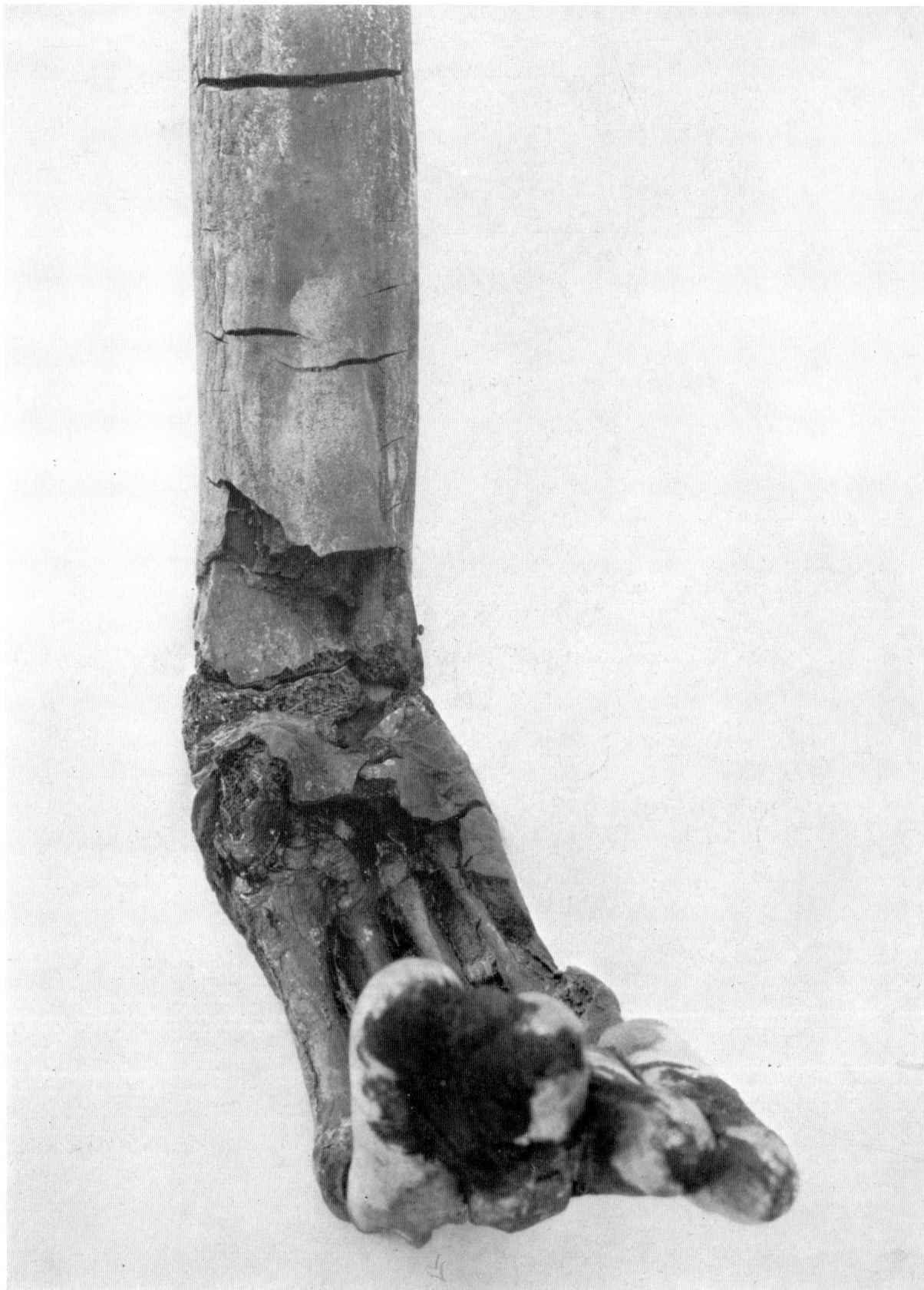

The Royal Mummy: the right hand and forearm
Photograph by Harry Burton. Griffith Institute

PLATE XVII

The Royal Mummy: the right hand and forearm disarticulated

Photograph by Harry Burton. Griffith Institute

PLATE XVIII

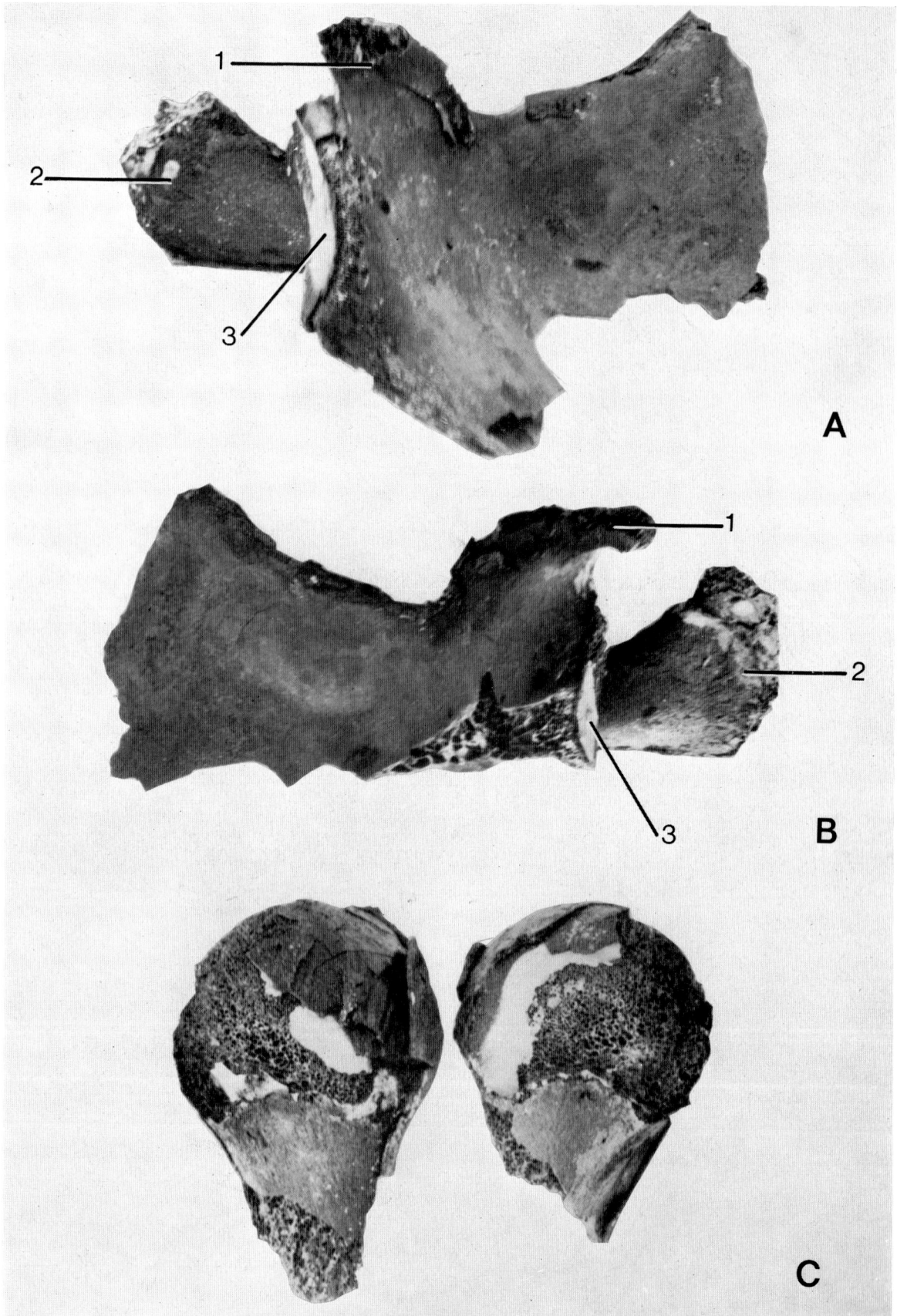

The Royal Mummy: parts of the scapulae, and the heads of the humeri
Photograph by Harry Burton. Griffith Institute

PLATE XIX

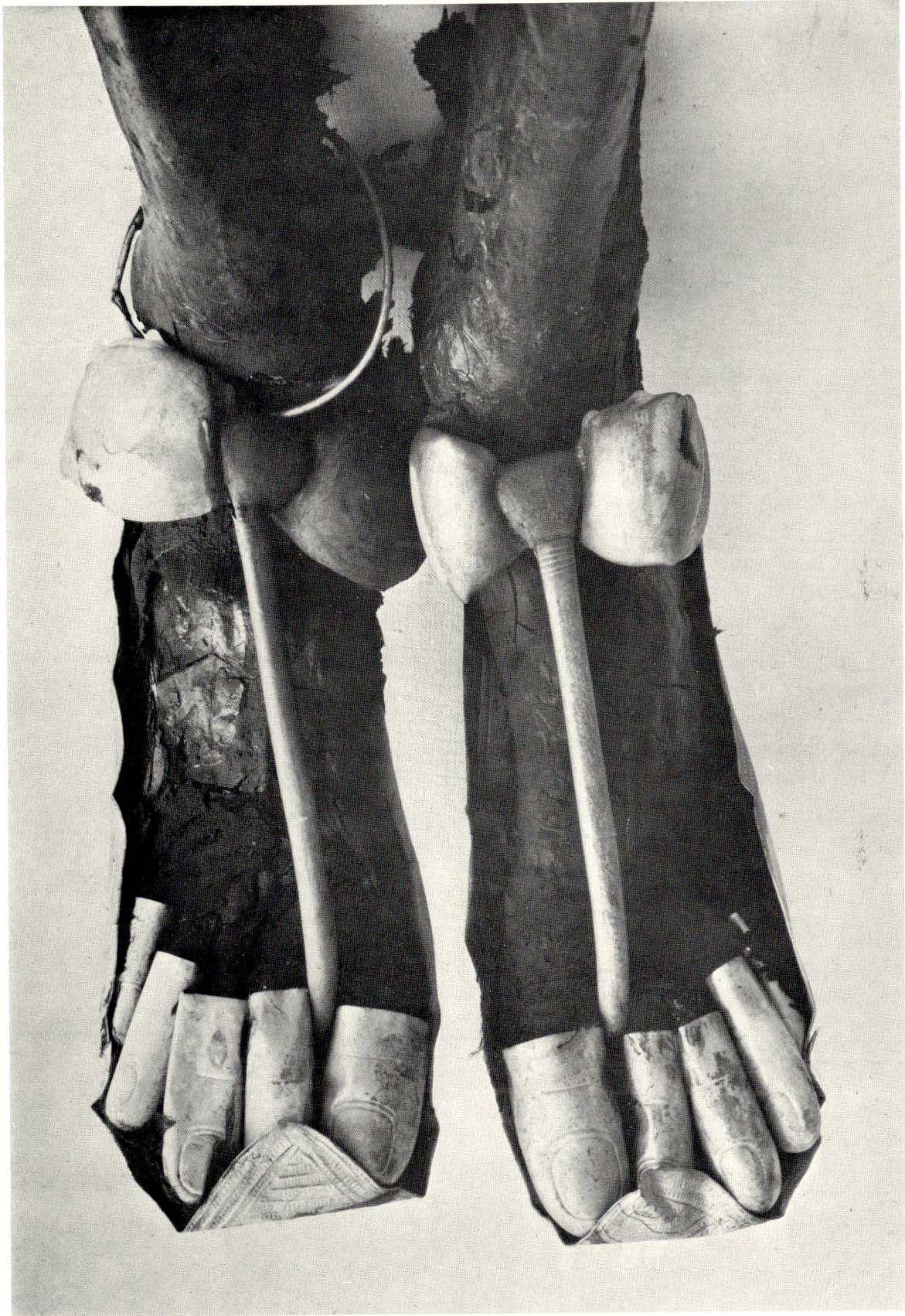

The Royal Mummy: the feet

Photograph by Harry Burton. Griffith Institute

PLATE XX

The Royal Mummy: the body unwrapped
and reassembled
Photograph by Harry Burton. Griffith Institute

PLATE XXI

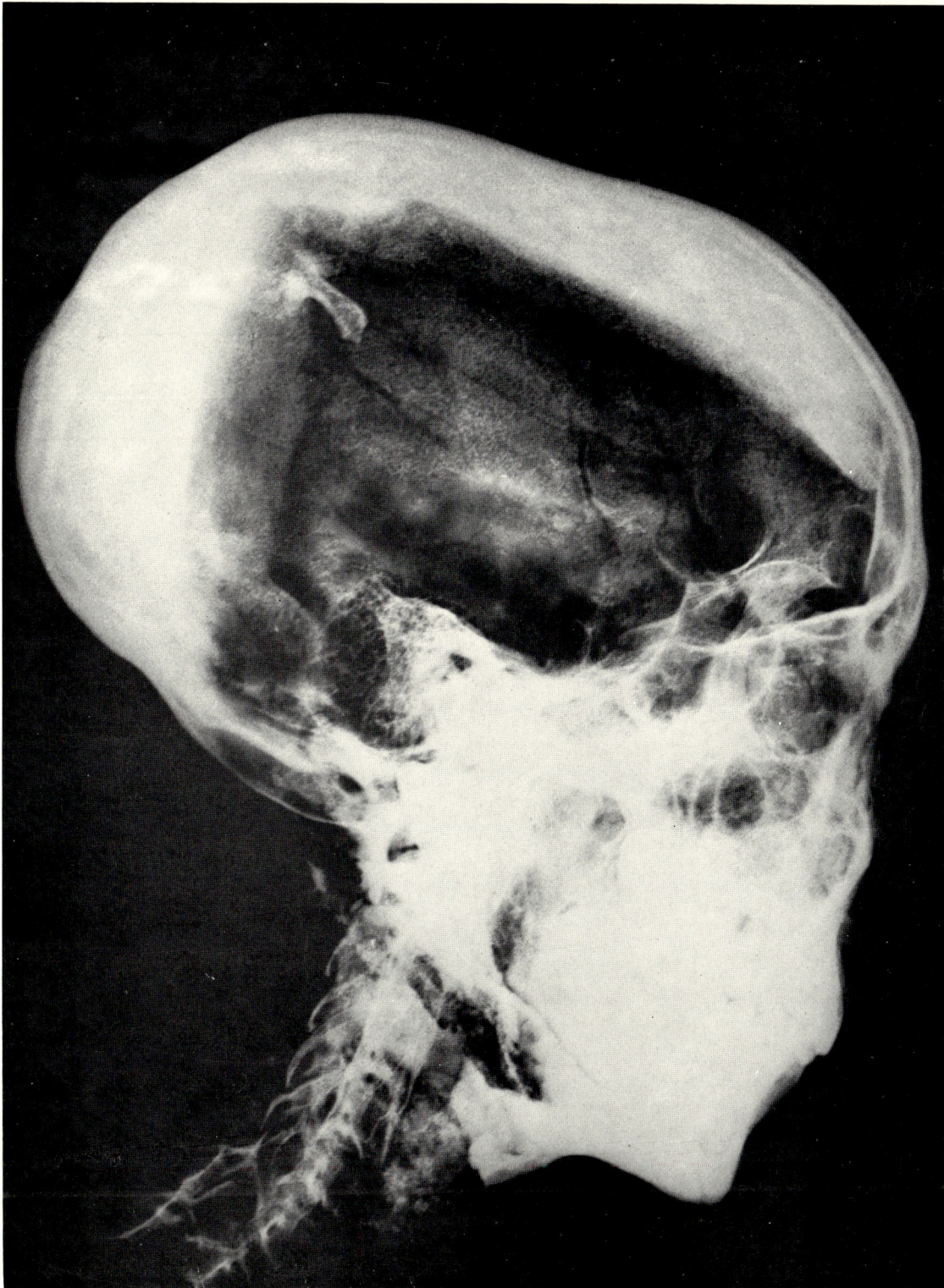

The Royal Mummy: lateral X-ray of the head
Photograph copyright *The Times*

PLATE XXII

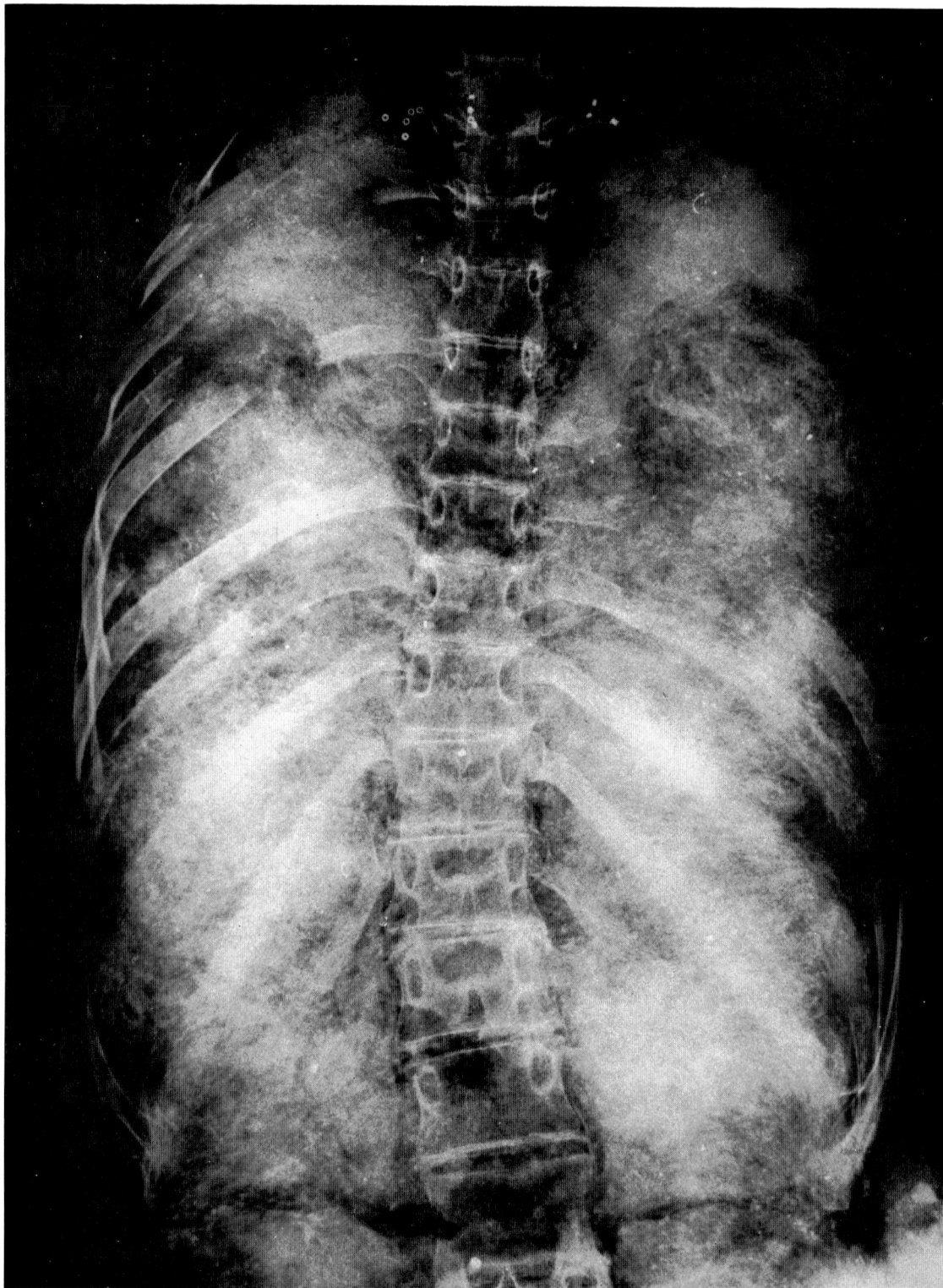

The Royal Mummy: X-ray of the trunk
Photograph copyright *The Times*

PLATE XXIII

317 *a* (2)

317 *b* (2)

The mummies of the two foetuses in their respective coffins
Photographs by Harry Burton. Griffith Institute

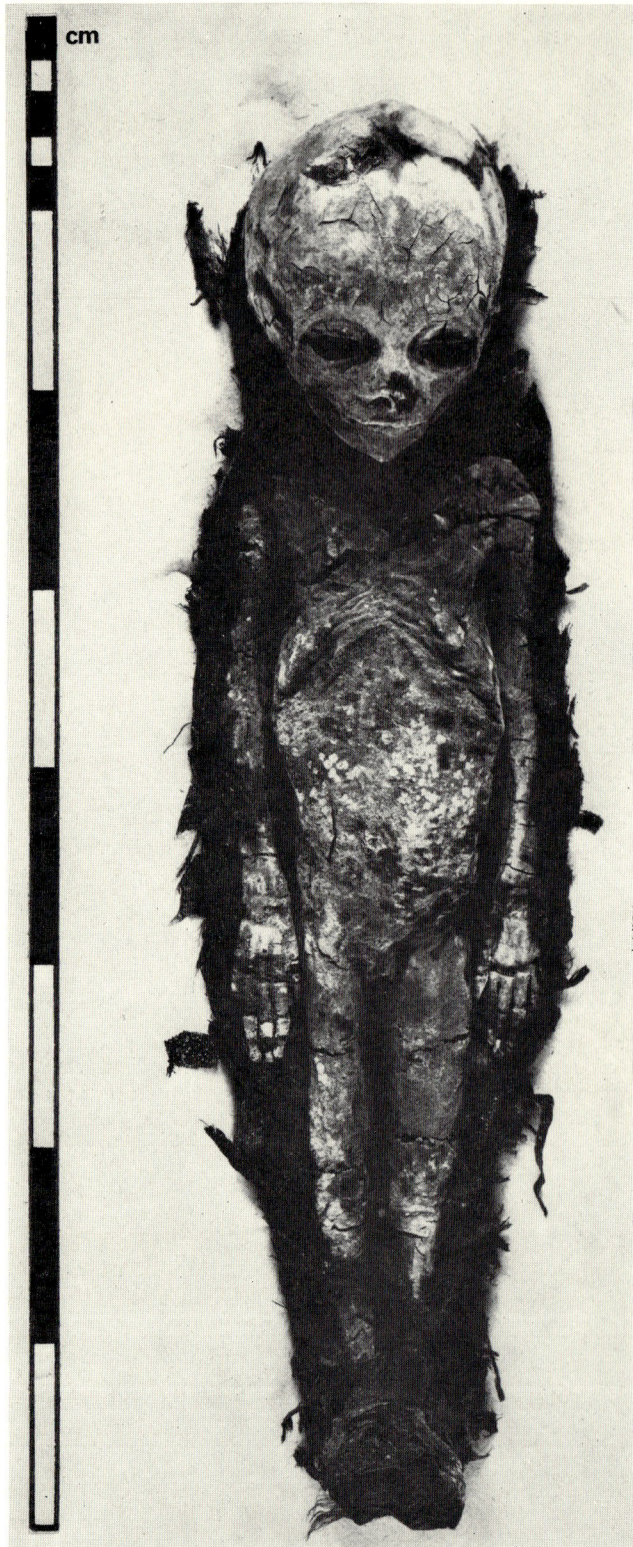

PLATE XXIV

317 a (2)

317 b (2)

The two foetuses after unwrapping

Photographs by Harry Burton. Griffith Institute